MAKING THE MOMENT MEANINGFUL
Creating a Path to Purpose and Fulfillment

Dana LaMon

ImageWorth
2011

ImageWorth
P.O. Box 6108
Lancaster, California 93539-6108
(661) 949-7423
www.makingthemomentmeaningful.com

ISBN: 978-0-9656633-1-1
Ebook: 978-0-9656633-6-6

LaMon, Dana, 1952-
    Making the moment meaningful: creating a path to purpose and fulfillment / Dana LaMon.
        p. cm.
    LCCN 2011907142
    ISBN-13: 978-0-9656633-1-1
    ISBN-10: 0-9656633-1-0
    ISBN-13: 978-0-9656633-6-6
    ISBN-10: 0-9656633-6-1

    1. Self-actualization (Psychology)   I. Title.

BF637.S4L36 2011   158.1
                        QBI11-600127

Cover design: Jill Goodmon, Goodmon Graphics

Printed in the United States of America
First ImageWorth Printing: August 2011.

For Sharon
and
for all who feel the yearning for meaningfulness.

The best cause requires a good pleader.
                    - Dutch Proverb

MAKING THE MOMENT MEANINGFUL
Creating a Path to Purpose and Fulfillment

TABLE OF CONTENTS

CHAPTER

PART I:
WHAT LIFE IS ABOUT

PART II:
PROMOTING GROWTH

PART III:
ESTABLISHING AND NURTURING CONNECTION

PART IV:
DISCOVERING PURPOSE

PART V:
DEFINING YOURSELF

PART VI:
WHAT GETS IN THE WAY

PART VII:
THE COMMITMENT TO MEANINGFULNESS

PART VIII:
THE SATISFIED LIFE

Happiness requires something to do, something to love and something to hope for.

- Swahili Proverb

PART I:
WHAT LIFE IS ABOUT

A man should live if only to satisfy his curiosity.
- Yiddish Proverb

CHAPTER 1
YEARNING TO BE SIGNIFICANT

This life is your one opportunity to shape the world in which you live.

Early in 2006, I received a letter from a friend's husband who was ruminating over what to do with the second half of his life. He wrote that what he would do was not clear, but he was certain it had to be significant—something larger than himself.

Two years later, I had a telephone conversation with my friend herself. The topic? She struggled with the question of what to do with her life. She was working but wasn't sure if her job was where she should be spending her time. She worried about retirement—that is, not having enough resources set aside in order to live in her retirement years.

My friend and her husband are not alone. Over the years, I have had several conversations with people who desired to "do something meaningful" or "make a difference" or "leave a legacy." Books have been written with the intent of answering the question, "What should I do with my life?"

One morning not too long ago, I turned on the radio to listen to my regular public radio station, and they were doing a story about a woman in Minnesota who was selling everything she owned, keeping only her important papers, and driving west to find a simpler life. She acknowledged that the things she owned didn't make her happy. She believed that a life uncomplicated with things would allow her to find the happiness she sought.

The yearning to feel significant is experienced by people who have done little with their lives up to now and by those who can tout a long list of achievements. Success in the form of wealth, position, status, or fame has not satisfied this longing to matter.

Why is it that we wait until we have lived a half century or so before we decide to do something that we can label as significant? Does the yearning only begin then? Is it that we begin to think that our time is running out? Is it that we lose our amusement with the capitalistic carousel? Is this mid-life angst just a reflection of our voracious appetite for bigger and better?

Do you feel the yearning?

You were born to be significant. This life is your one opportunity to shape the world in which you live. You can choose to be a volunteer and shape your world to your specifications, or you can be a victim and let circumstances dictate your design. You can choose to ensure your significance in this world for your whole life or only for a part of it. That is to say, you don't have to wait until much of your life is past before thinking about the legacy that you leave. The earlier you begin to live meaningfully, the greater the impact you make on your world.

You can never know how long, when measured by time, your life could be. You did not enter this world with a guarantee of time. You may be around for another fifty years, and there are those whose lives lasted less than fifty seconds. Fortunately, the significance of life isn't judged by its length. Significance is determined by the meaningfulness of the time you spend. Your activities and actions and the motivation for them are relevant to meaningfulness regardless of how much time you feel you have left in life.

Life is short when measured by the things you can do with it. There are so many things you can do and certainly not enough time to do them all. The challenge, then, is to choose your actions and activities meaningfully. You must develop the decision-making skill to enable you to say yes to the things that matter and no to those that are of little importance. Every moment you give to insignificance diminishes your life's value. If you devote forty to fifty years of life to things that don't matter, you will have missed so much of life that could be lived fulfilling the yearning for significance.

You were born to be significant, and this innate instinct can be ignored only for a short time. If you live long enough to get past the social norms of getting an education, landing a job, starting a family, and/or acquiring possessions, the yearning to be significant will emerge in the question, Now what? You may respond to the question by repeating the cycle, believing that doing more satisfies the yearning. So you get another degree. Maybe you find a job that pays more money or carries more prestige. Perhaps you have another child to add to the family. You may buy more and/or bigger things. Despite doing and having more, the yearning is still there.

Unable to satisfy the yearning with more, you may seek fulfillment by having something different. You move. You change professions. You get divorced and, perhaps, remarry. Still there is a sense of dissatisfaction.

Now time has passed, you are older, and you begin to feel your mortality. The feeling of mortality serves to intensify the yearning to be significant.

Eventually this yearning to be significant will push its way to the point of priority and urgency. It may happen after your children have all grown up and left home. The yearning is then expressed as the "empty nest syndrome." It may happen when you retire and a day-to-day job is no longer in the way. You may then begin to question your worth because your work was where you placed your importance. It may happen during a financial hardship when you've lost your job and/or lost the things that have occupied your mind and time. You begin to learn that things don't matter.

The instinct for significance is always present. When rearing children, working a job, tending to things, and other business no longer suppress it, you will hear its cry and feel its yearning. You need not wait—and should not wait—until much of your life is behind you before you begin your quest to discover what will satisfy the yearning. The way to maximize the significance of your life is to make each moment meaningful from the beginning. Choose a course of education that highlights your talents and abilities, not the one that just heightens your earning potential. Make parenting a meaningful experience for you, your partner, and your children. Seek employment with more than just making money in mind. Don't rest your identity and your value in your possessions. Establish a view of your life that allows you to see clearly what is meaningful and augments your living. Then you can avoid the things that consume and waste the precious little time that you have to shape your world.

CHAPTER 2
MEASURING THE MOMENT

The value of life must be measured, not by the minutes, but by the moments.

I was twenty-seven years old before I attended a funeral. A friend living in Connecticut asked that I be with her for her mother's memorial service. With one day's notice, I flew from California to be with Penny at her time of grief.

More than thirty years have gone by and I have attended over forty services to honor the life of members of my family, friends, and cohorts. I have spoken at nearly half of them. My first opportunity to speak at a funeral was in 1980. It was for Norman, who was killed in the cross fire of two rival gangs while spending an afternoon in the park. I presented a message, not to Norman, but to the hundreds of young teens who mourn the death of a sixteen-year young man, about the need to put guns down.

Quite the contrast was the memorial service for Shortie. I came to know her through our membership in Toastmasters International, an organization with a focus on improving speaking skills. Shortie's memorial was not a time of mourning; it was a celebration of a life. My heart wells up with emotion and my eyes often with tears when I recall the gesture initiated by the minister. Recognizing that ninety percent of the people present were members of Toastmasters, she asked that we give Shortie her final standing ovation.

At Annie Mae's memorial service, her children talked about the love they received from their mother. The recurrent theme was that none of the eight children remembered their mother saying "I love you," but never did they have a doubt that she did. Her family believed that their mother lived love.

Annie Mae being one of my cousins, I learned something about myself and my family and how we express love.

Dennis' family did not speak at his funeral service. We instead heard from Dennis' cell mates. All shared stories of a man "who would give you the shirt off his back." I delivered the eulogy for this forty-something man and incorporated stories from his siblings to talk about the value of the life that Dennis shared. After the service, a man whom I did not know asked for my business card so I could be called to deliver his eulogy. He said, "Man, when I die, I want you to talk at my funeral 'cause you made Dennis look good."

Many of the obituaries of the people whose services I attended contained a line that described the span of the person's life. The line might read: "Candy lived thirty-seven years, three months, two weeks, and five days."

How will your life be measured?

Life...your life...is that segment of eternity during which your soul, mind, and body join to interact with the universe. It is commonly understood as the time that you are born to the instant of your death. Your mother, the doctor, and all the people around you began measuring your life by seconds, minutes, and hours; days, weeks, and months; then years. In the minds of most people, life becomes time.

Life...your life...has no defined length until it is over. It could have been as short as one second; it can be longer than one hundred years. Because it has no defined length, there is no way for you to know if you have done something to make it longer. You cannot say that you have added days to your life unless you know when it was supposed to end. You can believe—and should believe—that if you promote the health of your body and protect yourself from injury, you will prolong life. The value of your life, however, is not in the length of it.

You had nothing to do with the segment of eternity in which your span of life has encompassed. You are here now, but you could have come in prehistoric times, medieval times, or lunar times (the time when man will inhabit the moon). The value of your life is not judged by the period in which you live.

If you think of life as time—as the seconds, minutes, or hours that pass—the significance of life is diminished. The clock becomes the force that dictates what you do. You are manipulated, managed, and motivated by the hour. You become satisfied with terms such as "rush hour" and "happy hour" to define your activities. You willingly and wantonly "bide time," "waste time," and "kill time" as though you have plenty of it to spare.

When you measure the significance of your life by the calendar, you are likely to dread Mondays, applaud "hump day," and celebrate Fridays. You may adopt as your theme song "Living for the Weekend." You can't wait for the long weekends or your two-week vacation. You set aside a special day on the calendar to show love, to give thanks, or to appreciate your mother and father.

If you become complacent about life and think of it only in terms of time, it may take an alarming event to wake you up. You might awaken to the brevity of life if you have a close connection with someone who dies at a young age. You might awaken to the importance of making the moment meaningful if you experience a life-threatening illness. All along you know that you are mortal, at least subconsciously if not consciously, but you always expect there to be tomorrow. There is nothing wrong with having such hope of the future days of your life. However, you should never squander this present moment on the expectation that you will have another one.

The clock and the calendar are meaningless gauges of life. Life must be measured, not by the minutes or the months, but by the moments. A moment is the span of your

life given to a specific experience. Just as life has no pre-
defined length, a moment is indefinite. The duration of a
moment can be a second or a lifetime. It coincides with the
duration of an experience that you have.

Because it encompasses an experience, a moment has
three dimensions—physical, mental, and spiritual. The
physical dimension of a moment is length, which is measured
by time. The mental dimension of a moment is breadth,
which is measured by knowledge the experience gives you.
The spiritual dimension of the moment is depth, which is
measured by the impact you have on others. If you are living
a life that simply marks off time and is governed by the
calendar, you are living a one-dimensional life. You can
never experience the fullness of life in one dimension. The
meaningfulness of your life must be measured by the breadth
and depth of your moments.

The moment of utmost importance is Now. Now is the
point at which your past connects with your future. This
connection provides the continuity of your experiences that is
your life. If this continuity is broken—that is, if Now no
longer exists, then life ends. Hence, Now is the moment you
live and make life meaningful.

Now is the intersection of multiple moments. It may be
the end of some experience. It is the continuation of other
experiences. It must be the beginning of new experiences if
tomorrow is to have meaning for you.

You can exercise control over the three reference points
of life—past, present, and future. However, the tools by
which you exercise control are different. You control the past
with memory. You control the present with action. You
control the future with planning.

CHAPTER 3
LEAVING YESTERDAY BEHIND

You must leave yesterday behind but extract from it two things—memories and lessons.

In my brief career practicing law in California, I handled marriage dissolutions. I encountered no two marital relationships that were the same. John and Jamie, fundamentalist Christians who married each other in their fifties, could not get along after two years of being wedded. Mary, who was seventy-nine years old, hired me to terminate her five-year marriage to her husband of the same age. Melanie and Larry, a young couple that had not yet been together for five years, battled over custody of their two-year-old son as they decided to go their separate ways. Veronica had to quit her job and leave the state to hide from Mark, who threatened to shoot her and her coworkers because he didn't want to divorce. Brenda destroyed Walter's car, house, and clothes as she took custody of their three children and exited the marriage. I quickly wearied of handling conflicts between couples who could no longer get along.

Though the particulars of each marriage break-up were different, I observed in each relationship disappointment and/or frustration that marriage was not what the individuals expected.

I was a single man when I practiced law, so I had no practical marriage experience, only a vision of what a successful marriage should be. Included in my ideal was how I would approach a marital relationship that was no longer viable. Maybe because of the personal conflicts I witnessed, I resolved that she, whoever she might be, could have the property and custody of the children. I'd want my after-marriage relationship to be as free from my ex-wife as possible.

I did not try to impose my ideal on my clients. I carried out my client's wishes as his or her legal representative. Even when Brenda sought one hundred percent of the property and sole custody of the children, a position contrary to California law, I argued it before the judge. Because of the evidence we presented on trial, she, at least temporarily, got almost all that she sought. But then she got all the headaches that come with continual contact with a non-cooperative ex-husband.

What about yesterday can you change?

Your life of yesterday is carved in stone. You cannot change it. You cannot relive yesterday. You cannot pretend that the past did not happen. Well, yes you can, but pretending that it did not happen does not change what yesterday is. Mourning over the past or ruminating about what-ifs will only cause you to miss the opportunity to make the most of today.

Yesterday will remain forever in the past. The only part of the past that you can bring to the present moment is the memories and lessons of your past experiences. If you have memories of past experiences that brought you joy, be grateful for them. Cherish them. Share them readily. These are the moments that make life meaningful. Be careful, however, that your celebration of yesterday's joyful memories do not supplant the actions to be taken to make the moment now meaningful. Memories will lose their meaningfulness if they thwart forward motion.

If yesterday is full of experiences that gave you pain, use the moment now to soothe the pain and heal. Dwelling on the past will keep the pain in the forefront of your mind and delay the healing process. Observe what you lost and begin your efforts to replace or compensate for it. Make a note of what you might have done to bring about the painful experience, and learn from your error so that you don't repeat it. Identify who or what contributed to the negative experience and separate yourself from her, him, or it now so that today isn't a repeat of yesterday.

To know pain, you must experience pain. Yesterday's experiences may have caused you pain, but you should use the experience of pain as a lesson learned about what to avoid today and tomorrow.

To leave yesterday behind does not mean forgetting it. Recall the situations that produced those pains, analyze the situation, and learn from the lessons they teach so you can avoid similar pains in the future.

Leaving yesterday behind does depend on your ability to forgive. You cannot make the best of the moment now if you are carrying around guilt from yesterday's actions. After you acknowledge your responsibility for yesterday's experiences, release yourself. Yesterday is gone, and your part is complete. To release yourself, you must forgive, apologize, and restore. Forgive yourself for mistakes of omission or commission and focus on the role you must play now. You must then apologize for harm you may have caused someone else. You cannot claim meaningfulness in a life that has caused pain to others and/or has been detrimental to another person's effort to live a meaningful life. Along with apologizing, you must offer restitution. To the extent that you can, compensate the individual for the losses you caused. Once you have apologized and provided restitution, consider yourself released and move on. If the person you harmed forgives you, you have no reason to continue carrying a burden of guilt. If they are not willing to forgive you after you have offered your sincere apology, the burden shifts to them. They have chosen to carry it, so you should let it go.

By the same token, you must be willing to forgive the person who may have been responsible for the painful experience you lived yesterday. When you are not willing to forgive, you choose to carry the weight of the matter into the present moment. While someone else may be responsible for what you experienced yesterday, you are the one responsible for reliving the pain today.

If there is something about yesterday that merits reliving, live it now, but do so only if there is not something greater to be attained. Otherwise, let now be the period of your life to go and grow beyond yesterday's achievements.

If any part of yesterday was wasted on things that have no meaning for you, don't worry about it. It's now gone. Spending life now regretting time wasted in the past, wastes the present and the future, making the moment meaningless.

CHAPTER 4
MAKING THE MOST OF TODAY

*You get the most out of life today when you feel the urgency
of now with equal intensity as the expectation of tomorrow.*

Bob Koken is eighty-nine years old. He retired thirty
years ago after working thirty years for General Electric as a
mechanical engineer. While he has retired from going to a
job, Bob has not retired from living.

Every day of his very active life, Bob has breakfast with
a friend—not the same person each day, but different friends.
Just about every day he talks to his sisters on the phone. One
is a year younger and the other six years older. Everyday he
reads the newspaper and the book of his choosing. Once a
week Bob volunteers at a preschool for children who have
been abused. Two or three times a month he visits people in a
home for senior citizens and sings and recites poetry. Bob
helps persons with mobility limitations by providing free
loans of wheelchairs and scooters. He currently has more
than twenty of them out on loan. He bought magnification
equipment for a friend in Arkansas who was losing her sight
and software for a blind man to enable him to read printed
material with his computer.

Bob is happy with what he is doing. Whenever I ask
how he is doing, he responds, "Doing so well I almost feel
guilty." This is his response notwithstanding the fact that he
has impaired hearing and wears hearing aids, that he can't
drive at night because of limited vision, and he has a problem
with balance owing to a brain injury he sustained over forty
years ago.

I first met Bob in January 2005. We sat together on the
commuter bus. It was my usual ride from downtown Los
Angeles back to Lancaster, but it was not usual for him. He

usually took the Antelope Valley line of Metrolink from Union Station. The train was not running that afternoon because of a fatal collision with a train and an SUV. Bob was able to take the train in the morning to make his every-Wednesday visit with his now deceased brother, who was in a Long Beach convalescent home, but he had to take the bus as alternate transportation back home.

One might think that Bob, at his age, wouldn't have many more years to live. He told me in a recent telephone conversation that he feels good and expects to be around at least another ten years. That day he met a friend for breakfast, read a bit, made arrangements to buy another wheelchair, and talked with some of his children on the phone. Every day he is doing what gives him a sense of fulfillment.

What are you doing today that makes you happy?

The most important time of your life is now. It doesn't matter how many years are behind you or how many years you believe are ahead. You may be twenty-nine or eighty-nine years old. The time to make life meaningful is right now.

If you are a young person, you should resist the temptation of putting off meaningfulness for later in your life. Making a living should not take priority over making the moment meaningful. It is never too early for you to discover your purpose and then to seek the job that allows you to work purposefully. When you delay purposeful living, you are more likely to be distracted by things that don't matter. You also delay the meaningful impact your life can have.

If you are a person of mature years, you must not think that too much of your life has already passed to make life meaningful. You have today, and today offers you one more chance to fulfill the purpose uniquely assigned to you. Never discount the significance of now no matter how much lies in your past.

Of all the moments of your life—those of the past and those that will be—the only one over which you can be sure of exercising full control is the moment now. Over yesterday and tomorrow you can only control your attitude. You cannot take action in the past, nor in the future. Only today can you act, react, and make the choices that are governed by your attitude. To maximize meaning in your life, you must learn from yesterday, act today, and plan for tomorrow.

You make the past a significant element of a meaningful present by using it as a resource for knowledge. From your experiences—your actions, reactions, and interactions—you grow. You discover purpose. You nurture beneficial relationships. You define your beliefs and guiding principles. Learning from the past, today you can avoid actions of insignificance and meaninglessness. You cannot make the most of now if you continually repeat the acts of yesterday.

Now is the time to act. For what are you waiting? Are you waiting to finish school? Are you waiting to get a job? Are you waiting for money to come your way? Are you waiting to marry and to rear a family? Are you waiting to retire? Today you live. Life doesn't begin tomorrow. Going to school, working, and having a family are all part of life now. What you do to make a difference in this world should not be separate from your day-to-day activities. It is what you do now in school, what you do now in church, what you do now at home, and what you do now at the job that make the difference. The more you do now, the greater the difference you make.

Though tomorrow is not promised you, you should take time today to plan and prepare for it. Planning is a meaningful activity through which you create your opportunities for the future. Preparation readies you for the unexpected opportunities that may come a-knocking. If today you don't plan and prepare for the things that will matter to you tomorrow, you will likely spend your life on the things that don't matter.

The challenge is striking the appropriate balance between living today and planning tomorrow. With too much planning and not enough living, you will lose your chance to make the most of now. On the other hand, with too much living and not enough planning, you miss the opportunity to make the most of the future. You get the most out of life today when you feel the urgency of now with equal intensity as the expectation of tomorrow.

CHAPTER 5
APPROACHING TOMORROW

You can alter the quality and meaningfulness of your tomorrow by what you imagine and the reason you have to hope.

In January 2008, the management of the division in which I worked sent an e-mail to all employees announcing drastic changes that would be made in how we conduct business as a cost-cutting measure. We in the Los Angeles office were stunned by what we read. The proposed changes included closing the Los Angeles office, having judges to conduct hearings by videoconference in home offices that would be set up for each, and transferring all clerical positions to Sacramento. These changes were to take effect before the end of the year.

The proposal raised many questions that remained unanswered six months later. The proposal introduced into the lives of several an uncertainty about their future. While the changes wouldn't be immediate, employees' distant tomorrows were disturbed. The reactions to the disturbance were varied.

Collectively, the employees went into a resistive mode. They tried to reason with management by trying to show that the proposal didn't really save any money. They argued that the proposal violated the laws that protected the rights of the people we served. Finally, they went to outside sources to oppose management through the union and the legislature.

Individually, the reactions were of pain or resignation or both. One clerk cried for hours about needing her job to provide for her children. Another said that whatever happens she would deal with it when it occurred. All of the clerks began applying for other jobs. Only one actually left.

Judges in the office began serious discussions about retirement. One, who had already planned to retire in 2009, expressed his expectation that the change would not occur until after he was gone. A couple of others announced a date for retirement. Apparently unable to handle the stress of it all, three judges took medical leave.

I was stuck between a rock and a hard place. I wanted to fully support my colleagues. I did not want the clerks with whom I worked to lose their jobs. But I welcomed the idea of working from home at all times. I saw in the situation the possibility of doing more of what I do as an inspirational and a motivational speaker.

When it became evident that the proposal announced in January would likely not be implemented before the end of the year, the office settled back into an operational routine. There was still discussion from time to time about what would happen in the future, but there was little evidence of change of behavior.

How do you approach tomorrow?

Tomorrow is a concept of time yet to come that is the convergence of imagination and hope. Your body can never experience tomorrow. When it reaches that point that was tomorrow, it is today. You experience tomorrow through your thoughts and your emotions. You can alter the quality and meaningfulness of your tomorrow by what you imagine it can and will be and the reason you have to hope.

Tomorrow holds a treasure trove of possibilities. The wealth of what is possible tomorrow lies in the circumstances of tomorrow—the time, the place, the things, and the people. The depth and breadth of what you will find depends on the tools you use when you approach tomorrow. Here are some tools that may be used to mine the possibilities that lie in tomorrow.

Routine—that is, seeking tomorrow's possibilities in the repetition of the same set of circumstances as yesterday and/or today. You can approach tomorrow by setting your alarm to awaken you at the same time as you awoke today. You go through your usual morning rituals in getting dressed, eating, and preparing for the day's activities. You take the same route to the job to work with the same people and face the same issues you faced before. The calendar becomes the map that guides you to your possibilities. You may follow one routine Monday, Tuesday, Wednesday, Thursday, and Friday, and then follow another routine on the weekend.

Using routine as a tool to approach tomorrow, you will likely find the same possibilities tomorrow as you found today. The only chance that you will realize new possibilities is the occurrence of some unexpected event to push you out of the rut of your routine.

Memory—that is, seeking tomorrow's possibilities by resetting the circumstances to get the results you remember from the past. You can approach tomorrow's possibilities with the mindful certainty of what you have already experienced. You remember the good time you had last week, so you look forward to doing it again—whatever it was. You remember how she made you feel and you liked it, so you plan to see her again. As you plan for the re-encounter, you know that you may not be able to recreate the set of circumstances for the immediate tomorrow, but tomorrow's tomorrow or the one after that will suit you just fine. The benefit you got—financial, social, emotional, spiritual, or other—is worth the wait.

You can use memory as a tool for approaching tomorrow's possibilities to avoid what you don't want. Avoiding the times, places, things, and persons that annoyed, bothered, or hurt you becomes your way of mining new possibilities. You don't seek new possibilities; you just avoid some old ones. By chance, you may encounter something new.

Using memory as a tool to approach tomorrow affirmatively, you rely on certainty, the familiar, what you already know. The realm of possibilities in tomorrow is constrained by the limits of your memory and accuracy of your recall. If you can accurately recall and recreate the same set of circumstances, you will achieve what you set out to achieve—the same thing you got before.

Realism—that is, seeking to experience of tomorrow's possibilities only what you believe that you can handle. You can approach tomorrow's possibilities in the confines of your known resources and abilities. Do only what you have the money for because you don't know from where you might obtain other funds. Apply only for the job that specifies your qualifications instead of arguing that your qualifications would be comparable to what the employer is seeking. Look only for jobs in your area because you just bought the house you're living in. Meet only people who are like you—your age, your race, your political affiliation, and so on—because those are the people you are likely to get along with.

Using realism as a tool to approach tomorrow, you establish artificial limits on the possibilities. What is possible for you is only that which is logical...which makes sense...which is achievable. By setting these boundaries of realism, you seclude yourself from the vastness of innovation. Everything that exists today was once illogical, unreasonable, and/or unattainable in the minds of the general population. We know of it today because one day someone approached his or her tomorrow with a tool that allowed him or her to reach beyond realism for new possibilities.

Adventure—that is, seeking from tomorrow's possibilities something that you do not yet know or have not experienced. You can approach tomorrow's possibilities with a zeal for something new. You don't just wait for the unusual to happen, you plan for it to happen. You help create the set of circumstances that will result in a new experience. You are willing to meet new people, go to new places, and try new things.

Using adventure as a tool to approach tomorrow, you will likely find something different from what you encountered today. Your desire for these new encounters, however, is not just for the sake of the thrill, though adventure can lead you to be a slave to pleasure. As a tool for seeking tomorrow's treasure trove of possibilities, adventure is the way to expand your knowledge, uncover your hidden talents, develop your skills, establish new relationships, and discover ways to fulfill your purpose.

Attitude—that is, gauging the importance of your search for tomorrow's possibilities. You can approach tomorrow with the belief that whatever is going to happen will happen no matter what you do, or you can approach tomorrow with the belief that you have influence in determining the outcomes of the day. The belief that you have regarding your role in tomorrow's possibilities determines what tools you'll use to search out the possibilities. If you believe that you are just a pawn in a game that someone else is playing, you just wait for the circumstances to move you in one direction or another. If, on the other hand, you're the one playing the game, you devise the strategies and develop the tools that will ensure that you get what you are looking for.

Using attitude as a tool for approaching the possibilities of tomorrow is not optional. You will have an attitude about what lies in the future. You can choose whether to approach tomorrow as a routine or as an adventure. You have the option of using memory or realism as a tool to mine the treasures of tomorrow. On the other hand, your choice about attitude is not whether to use it or not to use it, but rather, what your attitude will be. You will approach tomorrow with an attitude and it will be yours, not the attitude of someone else.

Insight—that is, the ability to see the possibilities in whatever circumstances come with tomorrow. You can approach tomorrow with the confidence that whatever happens, you'll find something beneficial in the situation. Insight comes from an attitude that you have influence over what is possible for you. Living with such belief, you develop the habit of looking for your point of influence. The set of circumstances you confront are not intrinsically negative or positive. They are not good or bad. Positive, negative, good, bad, adverse, and beneficial are value judgments made about the situation. The value that you see or don't see in the circumstances is determined by your insight.

Using insight as a tool for approaching tomorrow ensures that you will realize the possibilities that are available for you tomorrow. You'll be certain that you can look at each day as one that enhances life.

Creativity—that is, making possibilities out of tomorrow's circumstances. You can approach tomorrow with an open mind ready to reshape the circumstances—i.e., people, places, and things—to fit your purpose. This means, of course, that you have to know your purpose or purposes. Your mind must be open so that there can be a free flowing of thoughts and ideas. Your sense of adventure, influential attitude, and insight guided by purpose gives you a perfect setting for not just searching for the possibilities, but creating them.

Using creativity as a tool for approaching tomorrow, you control the circumstances to open up possibilities. You set the time to do what you must do to achieve your purpose. You choose the people with whom to interact. You determine what things are important for tomorrow to be meaningful, and you decide where it will happen.

CHAPTER 6
CHOOSING TO LIVE MEANINGFULLY

There are too many things to do to fit into one lifetime.
Choose to do what makes life meaningful.

During the summer after my first year of law school, I obtained a job in the office of the Los Angeles City Attorney. I was assigned to handle incoming calls from the public to direct the caller to the appropriate unit of the office or to refer him or her to another government entity. Usually the City Attorney assigned this task to newly hired attorneys. Because the job was so onerous, a person was assigned to the "public desk" on a two-week rotation. I did it for two months. My success in performing the job prompted the City Attorney to offer me a full-time position. I was tempted to accept it. At the time I was receiving $313 a month in Aid to the Blind, so the $1,049 monthly salary that the City Attorney offered was enticing.

Before making my decision, I talked with Harvey, the friend who recommended that I attend law school. His advice was that I return to school instead of taking the full-time job. He warned that interrupting my educational pursuit might result in my never completing law school. I followed Harvey's advice and turned down the job offer.

However, my finishing law school at the University of Southern California was almost interrupted by my desire to be with Andrea. I was in love, or at least I thought I was in love with the young lady whom I met while attending Yale. She herself was not a Yale student but lived in New Haven where Yale is located. At the time that I was in law school, she was attending college in Boston. As much as my limited income would allow me to pay the telephone bill, I talked with her as often as I could. I loved her voice. I loved the way she made me feel when we talked. The pleasure of the relationship far surpassed the displeasure of law school.

I investigated transferring to Boston. I considered Boston College. The idea of transferring was stopped abruptly when Andrea offered a point of consideration. She suggested that I figure out what my problem was—whether it was external or internal. She remarked, "If your problem is inside you, you will bring it with you if you move to Boston."

I figured that the problem was just a matter of adjusting to the new geographic and academic environment. I faced the same adjustment issue in my first year at Yale, and I expected that moving to Boston would not have made adjustment any easier. I stayed in Los Angeles and addressed the matter there.

I didn't always have the wise counsel of a friend when choosing what actions to take. Sometimes my choices were driven by the desire for pleasure or recognition or revenge. Usually, my actions so driven were regrettable rather than meaningful.

How do you know when to say yes and when to say no to opportunities that present themselves to you?

Your life is the result of the choices you have made up to now. No matter what words you use to describe life, you will be expressing your assessment of what you have gotten from your past decisions. Life for you may be happy, unfair, wonderful, difficult, great, sucky, pleasant, depressing, peaceful, hard, meaningful, complex, joyful, hectic, sweet, ruined, satisfying, meaningless, exciting, the pits, or some other term that I can't write in this family-friendly book. You cannot change the decisions you have already made. You can, however, change your assessment of the results. You can also change the way you make your future decisions.

It is impossible for you to do everything. First, life is not long enough for that. Second, some things require knowledge, skills, and/or inclination that you may not have. Third, some things are mutually exclusive—that is, to do one thing excludes some other. Whatever options come your way, you must be able to decide if they're ones you should seize as opportunities to make life what you want it to be.

While you can't do everything, there are many opportunities that you can seize. Too many to fit into one lifetime. From among the many, many options available to you, you must choose. Whatever choice you make is a decision that the action or activity is important enough to give up your limited time. Once the time is spent, you cannot get it back.

To determine if your time—i.e., your life—is well spent, you must identify what you are getting in exchange. Are you exchanging life for things that are lasting or for things that provide only temporary satisfaction?

❖   *Are you getting money? Is it enough? How much more would be enough?*

❖   *Are you getting pleasure? Will the pleasure last a lifetime, or will you have to keep giving your life for a repeated thrill?*

❖   *Are you getting recognition? Is it from someone who loves you? What good is recognition from a person who doesn't care about you?*

❖   *Are you getting revenge? When you get revenge, are you really getting or are you losing?*

Life choices that are based solely on money, pleasure, recognition, and/or revenge are not likely to result in a sense of fulfillment. The gratification you get from attaining them doesn't last. You have to keep repeating the action or find new ways to generate the feeling of satisfaction that they provide.

The sense of fulfillment and meaning comes from the choices you make to positively impact your world. The impact you have can only be known after the choice is made. It would be too late to wait until the end of life to assess whether the choices you made were the best choices. Because you cannot relive your life with the knowledge and wisdom of the experiences you gained, you must develop a way of determining today whether the choices you make today are the ones that make life meaningful.

I offer four factors to consider when making your choices of what to do for lasting impact.

Growth. Ask yourself: If I do this, will it promote my growth and development? Every living thing is growing and developing. When it stops the development process, it starts dying. If what you choose to do is not leading toward your growth, it is pushing toward your demise and will not make life meaningful. (See Chapters 8 through 11.)

Connection. Ask yourself: If I do this, will it promote connection with the people around me and my environment? Will it establish or nurture mutually beneficial relationships? Your relationships with people add significance to life that your relationships with things cannot. When you interact beneficially with another individual, you enhance your life and hers (or his). If this mutual benefit does not exist, one of you is using the other. The used loses life with no gain. (See Chapters 12 through 16.)

Purpose. Ask yourself: In doing this, do I fulfill my purpose? The possessive "my" is important here. Fulfilling a purpose does not necessarily make your action meaningful. Fulfilling your specific purpose does. Every element of creation serves a purpose. You differ from inanimate objects of the universe and other living creatures in that you get to choose whether to live within or outside your purpose. You act meaningfully when you do what you were meant to do. (See Chapters 17, 18, and 19.)

Self-definition. Ask yourself: Will doing this be consistent with the principles that define me and that I have adopted as my guides? You have beliefs, standards, and principles that you have adopted. Though you may not have put them in writing and may not be able to articulate them, they are reflected in your actions. They define your attitudes and views—in short, your life. If you choose actions contrary to your defining principles, your beliefs, standards, and principles are empty and meaningless. If they are meaningless, so will be your life. (See Chapters 20 through 23.)

You can maximize the meaningfulness of your life by choosing to do that which promotes your growth, establishes and nurtures connection, fulfills your purpose, and is consistent with the beliefs that define you.

No matter how far you have gone on a wrong road, turn back.

- Turkish Proverb

CHAPTER 7
IMAGINING A MEANINGFUL LIFE

The image that you hold in your mind of the life that you want to live is the context in which you respond to opportunities.

As we sat in a restaurant having lunch together during my last year of law school, Harvey, my high-school chum and college mate, engaged me in conversation about my plans for practicing law.

"What kind of law do you want to practice?" Harvey asked. "What do you see yourself doing as a lawyer?"

I responded, "I don't know for sure. I don't see myself arguing one side of a case or the other. I see myself sitting on the bench and making the decision."

The picture of my being a judge that was evoked by Harvey's questions stuck with me. Within five years, I was doing what I pictured myself doing albeit not in a courtroom.

In 1980, I was working as the executive director of the Disabled Resources Center in Long Beach, California. It was my third job following law school. A job announcement crossed my desk. It was from the Department of Social Services. This State of California department was seeking applicants for the position of Hearing Officer, the precursor classification for the current administrative law judge position. They were affirmatively seeking applicants who had a disability. As the executive director of DRC, it was my responsibility to pass the recruitment information to the counselors who could then identify clients for whom the job might be appropriate. Based on the description of the job— conducting quasi-judicial hearings concerning issues in social services programs, I decided it was a job for which I should apply.

It was easy for me to make the decision to apply for the hearing officer position. I had a picture in my mind of what kind of work I wanted to do with my law school training. With such a picture, I had no problem identifying a fitting opportunity.

What do you see as the picture for your life?

The image that you hold in your mind of the life that you want to live is the context in which you respond to opportunities. You should say yes to those opportunities that will complete the picture that you imagine of a good life and no to those that will not. At times you may find yourself saying yes when you should say no. In such situations, you are likely to regret the decision you made. You might even complain that life just is not going your way.

If you don't hold an image for your life, then you will struggle with your decision making. You will always be perplexed with whether to say yes or to say no. Even after you make the decision, you may be nagged with questions of uncertainty about your choice.

To be sure that you are making the decisions that will make your life meaningful, you must have an image of what a meaningful life is. This is not to suggest that you cannot live meaningfully without a vivid image of a meaningful life. It is possible for you to chance upon meaningfulness. The significance of having an image is a policy against making decisions that waste your life on activities that are insignificant.

What you envision as a meaningful life may not be the same as that imagined by your spouse or close friend or me. Your picture of life is drawn from your collection of experiences, complex of emotions, and vault of knowledge. Your experiences are not the same as mine; your emotional reactions are not the same as mine; your fund of knowledge is not the same as mine. Hence, there can be no question that what we draw from our differing resources will vary. Nevertheless, I share with you what I picture as a meaningful life to stimulate your creative thinking.

For me, a meaningful life is one that has the following benefits, opportunities, and responsibilities:

Basic needs for physical survival are met. It should be obvious that an essential element of meaningful life is life. Hence, we must have the things that sustain life—food, water, clothing, shelter, exercise, rest, etc.

Access to the universe of knowledge. Knowledge is the fuel for thought, ideas, and creativity. It is essential to the vitality of the mind as food is to the body. Since knowledge is not depleted when it is shared, we all can and should have equal access to the universe of what can be known.

To be loved. Love is the connective force of meaningful relationships. It provides the sense of belonging and appreciation that are crucial to emotional well being.

To love without inhibition. The natural tendency of love is to be shared. It is strengthened when it is allowed to flow. When the flow of love is thwarted, the result will be frustration, indifference, and apathy. A meaningful life should be one that is free from the barriers to expressing one's love.

Freedom to share what you think. One's thoughts are one aspect of a person's identity. You must be free to reveal who you are if your life is to be meaningful. This is not to suggest that a person with a mental illness or mental impairment cannot live a meaningful life. I make a distinction between freedom to express and ability to express. Meaningfulness is not a function of capacity but rather of opportunity without restriction by another person.

Freedom to express what you feel. One's emotions are another aspect of a person's identity. Like your thoughts, you must be free to reveal who you are if your life is to be meaningful. Again, I make a distinction between freedom to express and ability to express.

Freedom to decide what you do. Of the various and sundry activities to occupy your life, you decide which to do. Life cannot be meaningful for you if someone else controls what you should be deciding. You may grant another person the authority to decide for you because he or she is in a better position to make the decision. For example, the other person may have more knowledge regarding the situation and can, therefore, better assess the pros and cons of an action. So long as such delegation is willingly made, you are still in control.

To be forgiving. You have to be able to let go of offenses against you. Guilt, grudges, revenge, and retaliation are burdens that consume energy that can be used in moving ahead. If you forgive and let go, you avoid the chance of building barriers that interrupt the flow of love, and you ensure that your talents and abilities are not used to interfere with the meaningful life of another individual.

To discover your talents and abilities. The innate talents you have and the skills that you develop are the tools by which you serve your world. If you have not identified your talents and abilities, you miss the opportunity to add your uniqueness to the universe of good. If we don't use the talents given to us, everyone loses the benefit that could have come from them.

To use your talents and abilities toward meaningful living for others. You may discover that someone is willing to pay for your talents and abilities. However, money is not a gauge of meaningfulness. Life has meaning when you use your abilities to develop the meaningfulness of the life of another person.

Living does not interfere with or diminish the meaningfulness of another person. A meaningful life is not a life in isolation. What we do impacts the life of someone else. Your life assumes the value of your negative intention—that is, if you intend to have a negative impact, then your life is negative. If you intend to have a positive impact, the meaningfulness of your life is not diminished by unintended negative results.

Once you have developed your picture of a meaningful life, you have the framework for making each moment meaningful. You are the one who must take the initiative to do it. Here are the steps that this book leads you through to make the moment meaningful:

- ❖ Understanding Growth as a factor of meaningfulness (Chapters 8 through 11).
- ❖ Understanding Connection to others as a factor of meaningfulness (Chapters 12 through 16).
- ❖ Understanding Purpose as a factor of meaningfulness (Chapters 17 through 19).
- ❖ Understanding Self-definition as a factor of meaningfulness (Chapters 20 through 23).
- ❖ Recognizing the distractions to a meaningful life (Chapters 24 through 28).
- ❖ Encountering life as a three-dimensional being (Chapter 29).
- ❖ Evaluating your current actions and activities (Chapter 30).
- ❖ Determining what you want to do (Chapter 31).

❖ Assessing the meaningfulness of what you want to do (Chapter 32).

❖ Pursuing what you want in order to make life meaningful (Chapter 33).

❖ Considering how others will remember you (Chapter 34).

❖ Clearing out the clutter that is in the way of meaningfulness (Chapter 35).

PART II:
PROMOTING GROWTH

If we wonder often, the gift of knowledge will come.
— Arapaho Proverb

CHAPTER 8
MEANINGFULNESS: GROWTH

*Your potential for growth can be measured by the fervor of
your desire to try something new.*

There was a time in my life—I was about thirty-five
years old—when I considered myself to "have it made." I
had completed my educational goals—graduated from
college with a bachelor's degree, completed law school, and
passed the bar. I had a prestigious and well-paying position
as an administrative law judge. I was married to Jaci, an
intelligent and beautiful woman; we had two children. We
owned our home. I had achieved all the aspirations I had
imagined for my life. They were dreams and aspirations that
were developed out of societal expectations—graduate from
high school, go to college, get a job, get a wife, buy a house.

After I reached my goals, I fell into a routine of going to
work to "earn a living" and coming home to "raise a family."
My source of mental sustenance was TV; my spiritual health
depended on church routine. My rote living was interrupted
by a friend's request that I do something I had never done
before—give a humorous speech at his wedding.

When is it that we can say that we have it made?

You can say that you have made it when you reach the
ultimate goal of your life. What is that? What is the ultimate
goal of your life? It would be squarely contradictory to
believe that the ultimate goal of life is death. Death is simply
the end of your opportunity to attain another goal. (I have not
yet died, so I do not speak from experiential knowledge. The
latter assertion is what I surmise about death.) Until you

reach the end of life, you have the chance to achieve something else.

There is no ultimate goal of life. Once you achieve one goal, new life begins from that point. Your completion of high school or college is aptly referred to as graduation or commencement. You move on to the next stage; you begin a new course of life. The same is true about all your other achievements—employment, family, financial, etc.

Life is more than an alternating series of goals and successes. Achievement after achievement is meaningless unless you experience growth and development from what you do. Your capacity for growth depends on your amenability to change, your readiness to move forward, your hunger for knowledge, and your eagerness for new experiences.

Growth cannot occur without change. The process of growing and developing is a process of changing. If you fight or resist change seeking to stay where you are and doing what you do, you are fighting against growth. You are fighting against a factor that makes life meaningful. You can be actively involved in the creation of your enriched, enlightened, and meaningful life by accepting, inviting, and encouraging change.

Growth is manifested in forward progress. To move forward, you must be forward thinking. You must keep your mind open to allow for the free flow of thoughts and ideas and to allow for the reconsideration and reshaping of your beliefs as you gain new experiences. Forward progress requires that you position yourself so there is always room to move. Be flexible. Keep your options open. Forward progress is movement in the direction of the life that exposes, explores, and exhibits your talents and abilities. The ideal environment to allow for your forward motion is the place where you have an open mind, an open heart, and an uninhibited imagination.

Growth feeds on knowledge. When you have a hunger for knowledge and regularly feed it, your life is fattened with options and opportunities. If, on the other hand, you stop feeding your mind, or you feed it with junk that doesn't promote growth and development, your life will become emaciated. The sign of an emaciated life is one in which you always feel a sense of "barely making it" or "struggling to make it." The more you know, the more you grow.

Growth comes from new experiences. Your eagerness to do new things or to do old things in a new way provides the energy for growth and development. A new experience is a great source for knowledge. A new experience opens avenues for forward motion. A new experience is a catalyst for a changed life. Your potential for growth can be measured by the fervor of your desire to try something new.

Growth is a sign of life. When you stop growing, you have begun the process of death. You can forestall the process of dying by promoting your growth. Be a catalyst for change. Stay active. Keep learning. Try something new.

Unless you enter the tiger's den, you cannot take the cubs.
- Japanese Proverb

CHAPTER 9
CHANGING INTO YOU

Each new moment brings with it a new set of circumstances.
In each new set is another chance for you to move closer to
your goals.

She had the foresight that I would likely lose more of my sight, so the fourth-grade resource teacher required that I learn to type. She knew that even if I were blind, I could function in the world of sight if I could use a typewriter to communicate. I was not yet in the fourth grade, but Mrs. Somers wanted both Michael and me to get an early start in learning to use the typewriter keyboard. A couple of days a week we would spend our lunch break in Mrs. Somers' classroom with her new electric typewriters.

It was in 1961. I was in the third grade at McKinley Elementary School when I learned to use a typewriter. At the time I could see well enough to read large print, and McKinley had Sight Conservation classes where large print books were available.

Mrs. Somers guessed it right about me. I lost more sight, and before the end of my fourth-grade year, I was no longer able to read large print. I was transferred to Frances Blend Elementary School for the start of fifth grade where I learned to read Braille. My typing skills became useful when I got to junior high, high school, and college. While I obtained books in Braille and on tape, I had to type my tests and term papers to turn in to the teachers and professors, none of whom knew Braille.

What Mrs. Somers probably didn't imagine is that fifty years later I would be writing about her foresight using a keyboard like the one on the typewriter but connected to a computer that voiced the letters and symbols as I stroke the keys. I've adapted to the change from using my Remington manual typewriter to print my junior high school assignments to using a computer to write my administrative law judge decisions. Throughout much of the past forty years, the change has been gradual. I used my Remington typewriter through high school, Yale, law school at U.S.C., the bar exam, and my law practice. When I was hired by the State of California, I was given a Royal electric typewriter with which to write my decisions. I voluntarily began using a computer to write when I won an Apple II-C computer as a contestant on the *$25,000 Pyramid* game show. In 1991, I began using an IBM-compatible computer and WordPerfect 5.1 as a word processor. After that, technology accelerated the pace of change. I began resisting the change...well, I am still resisting. Here in 2011 I am still using WordPerfect 5.1 with MS-DOS. I'm just learning to use Microsoft Word.

How do you respond to change?

With every breath that you inhale, your body is changing. With every thought that you contemplate, your mind is changing. With every emotion that you feel, your spirit changes. As the seconds tick away, your environment changes. The change may be so gradual that you don't notice it, but it is happening. Though you may not see it as it occurs and you don't see it coming, you can look back and see its results.

Consider your life a year ago...five years ago...ten years ago...twenty years ago. You will observe the evidence of change. It is in your relationships, your profession, your skills, your knowledge, your opinions, your beliefs, your priorities, your bank account, your possessions, your hair. Things have changed in size or color or value or importance. You are not the same person you were two decades ago or ten years ago or five years ago or last year. The change that took place was necessary in order for you to become the person that you are today. Have you grown?

Change can be identified as external or internal, gradual or sudden, temporary or permanent, and negative or positive. Your ability to recognize these possible characteristics of change will help you to reap the greatest benefit from them. The benefit that you should always keep your eyes, ears, mind, and heart open for is growth. Every change that you see is either evidence of your growth or an opportunity for you to grow. It may be difficult for you to see the benefit in change, but if you trust that a benefit is there, you will keep looking for it. Of course, you must know what you benefit from in order to recognize the benefit when you see it.

An external change is one that occurs in your surroundings or environment. It is outside of you and outside of your control. Examples of external changes would include a change in the economy, in the weather, in the neighborhood, in the law, or in technology. Time is an external factor of change, so your reaching the age of twenty-one is an external change. Your moving from one place to another is an external change even if your move is voluntary because you do not control the specific characteristics of the surroundings to which you moved. Whether or not you find a benefit in change and grow from it will depend on your approach to external changes.

If your approach is to resist external changes, you will miss an opportunity to grow. When you resist change, you expend mental and emotional energy toward the end of keeping things the way they are...the way that is familiar and comfortable to you. Energy is wasted if it is used to keep you in the same place. The smart use of mental and emotional energy is to use it to move forward and/or upward. If you're feeling comfortable with where you are, you are probably not doing much growing. Growing and stretching makes you feel uncomfortable.

If you yield to external changes, you relinquish control of the direction of your life. You'll end up where the situation takes you, which could be to a place where you don't want to be. Placing your potential for growth in the hands of circumstances puts you in the position to be a victim if the situation isn't favorable to your interests, goals, and the meaningful life that you imagine for yourself. Even though you may not be able to control the situation, you can control your response to it.

When you adjust to external change, you may also lose an opportunity to grow. Adjusting is just shifting your position to keep doing what you are doing. You don't waste energy resisting the change, but you also don't look for the new opportunities that the change may bring.

When you celebrate external change, you place yourself in a position for maximum benefit and enjoyment from the things that come your way. Celebrating change is to treat it as a gift. Welcome it. Look carefully at it to see if it is what you have always wanted. If not, figure out how you can use it until what you desire comes along. To maximize the benefit from the gift you have been given, you have to know what you want and what purpose you wish to serve. The changed circumstances may not facilitate your universal or individual purpose, but it may benefit you in fulfilling an incidental purpose—a purpose for the time.

If you have a clear understanding and secure knowledge of your purpose and what you want to do with your life, you can approach external change by being a catalyst. You can assume an affirmative role in the creation of the circumstances that will ensure your growth and development. Being the catalyst does not mean necessarily that you can alter specific features of the circumstances around you. No human can change time or control the weather. You cannot change the people with whom you interact. As a catalyst, though, you can transplant yourself into situations that will represent a change in time or weather or relationships—a transplantation that better promotes your growth. You, on the other hand, may be able to change laws as a lawmaker, lobbyist, or petitioner. You may be able to change technology as an inventor. Being a catalyst of change may be your life calling; it may be the way you serve your environment and the people with whom you interact. In fulfilling your purpose, you also create the environment for you to grow.

An internal change is one that occurs with you and in you. Your internal changes can occur involuntarily due to external forces, and others come about voluntarily from your decisions and actions. Your body will age and change how it functions. Physically, you will not be able to do at age fifty what you did when you were fifteen. Through forces outside of your control and often without understandable reason, disease or disability may grip your body. Due to some physiological change, your mind may lose functional capacity. Despite these involuntary internal changes, you can still grow as a person. Your growth potential lies in the voluntary internal changes that you make—changes in your attitude, beliefs, actions, and reactions.

You can promote, and indeed speed up, your growing process by increasing your fund of knowledge. You open your mind to make room for and acquire information and ideas by reading; observing; researching; exploring; attending educational seminars and classes in person, on the internet, and/or by audio and video recordings; and discussing and debating issues. Your increased knowledge becomes fertile ground for new ideas and creativity.

The evidence of growth that comes from voluntary internal changes can be seen in your increased knowledge, wisdom and understanding, developed talents, and new or enhanced life and professional skills. You can control the direction of your growth in all of these areas. Knowing what you want, being willing to act in your best interest, and using your imagination, you determine if, when, where, and how you will develop and grow. Every time you grow in knowledge, wisdom, understanding, talent, and skill, you manifest yet another internal change. The new you provides the basis to promote further growth.

Changes that occur gradually are likely to cause you little problem or stress. You can yield to it without feeling that you are losing control. You can adjust to it with little effort to remain in the position with which you are comfortable. You can incorporate it into the day-to-day routine that you have established for yourself. With gradual change, however, you are likely to miss the opportunity to grow in unimaginable ways. Gradual change does not require you to take notice; it does not evoke imagination. What gets your attention is sudden change.

Sudden change—because it is unexpected and/or drastic—will incite fear in you. Fear is okay; it is a natural survival mechanism. If sudden change invokes in you the fear that prompts you to analyze the situation and run in the direction of survival, then you will grow. If, on the other hand, you fear sudden change to the point that you become immobile, you are likely to become a victim of change.

Temporary change, like gradual change, can work against your growing potential, especially if you know that it will be temporary. It will be easy to wait out the inconvenience until you can fall back into your comfortable position. A temporary change in circumstances can be a great opportunity for you to take a major risk on yourself. You have the security of knowing that if the risk does not pay off, you can get back to where you were before. A temporary layoff from a job, for example, is a fine opportunity to explore a new subject at a community college, spend some time on yourself—time you never seemed to have while you were working, or work on uncluttering your life of stuff. Obviously, you can do these things when a change is permanent, but in a temporary changed situation, you are less likely to experience the urgency of working to live.

There is a danger in labeling a change in your circumstances as positive or negative. In fact, no change is negative if from it you grow. Hence, you cannot rightfully label a change as negative until the situation is over. In calling it negative from the outset, you blur your ability to see the opportunity for growth in the new situation. Change is different, not positive or negative. If the different situation prompts you to do something different and/or to become someone different, it is a positive force toward growth.

Each new moment brings with it a new set of circumstances. In each new set is another chance for you to move closer to your goals. Each day you should look for the new opportunity and continue to move forward.

If you are moving along on the path of success that you have chosen for yourself and are enjoying life, you have managed to use change as a vehicle for growth and development.

Wood may remain ten years in the water, but it will never become a crocodile.

- Congolese Proverb

CHAPTER 10
LEARNING FOR A LIFETIME

Knowledge should not be obtained merely for the sake of having knowledge. It is not living knowledge if you hold it as a possession.

Shortly after I won Toastmasters International's World Championship of Public Speaking in August 1992, I received a call from Bob, a former vocational rehabilitation counselor from the California Department of Rehabilitation. Bob was my counselor for a couple of semesters while I attended Yale. After he had heard about my speaking award, he called me to ask if I'd be interested in giving a presentation at a conference to take place in October 1993—the California Disability Leadership Summit. He told me that the audience was expected to number over fifteen hundred. I agreed to do so. Bob said he would call me back with the topic and length of the speech.

I did not hear from Bob until I called him seven months later. Three weeks before the leadership summit, I called him to protest the topic I was assigned—"Diversity in the Field of Disabilities." I learned of the topic from a coworker in the Sacramento office of the State Hearings Division of the Department of Social Services. As we discussed a few matters related to hearings, he stated, "I see you will be speaking at the California Disability Leadership Summit next month."

"Where do you see that?" I inquired. Because I had not heard from Bob, I had concluded that perhaps he had changed his mind.

"It's in the brochure advertising the conference," my informant replied. He read me the section of the brochure regarding my speech.

"Bob, what have you done to me?" I asked in protest when I reached him on the phone. "Why do you have me speaking on diversity? I've never given a speech about diversity. I don't even know what the topic entails as it is addressed today. I hear people using the word, but I don't know the topic. So how can I talk about diversity in the field of disabilities?"

Bob responded calmly, "You're black. You're blind. You figure it out." Bob continued with some advice on how I should approach the subject. "You're scheduled to speak Wednesday morning, the last day of the conference. Get there on Sunday, the first day. Attend all the presentations you can. Listen to what people are saying in private conversations. Take the information you hear and prepare your presentation. You can do it."

More out of desperation than desire, I attended the conference from its opening session. I followed Bob's instructions and listened, listened, and listened. I had to somehow take my experiences as a black and blind man and relate it to men and women of various abilities and disabilities.

The speech was a success. It propelled me to a status of "expert"—in the eyes of some—on the subject of diversity in the field of disabilities. Within a year, I was presenting at a national conference on rehabilitation and diversity in Washington, D.C.

Are you still learning?

Learning should be a lifelong activity. It is the process of maintaining living knowledge. What you know is living knowledge if (1) it is a body of knowledge that is moving and growing and (2) it contributes to meaningful living.

Living knowledge is a vital element of personal growth. As your body of knowledge grows, so grows your field of opportunities and the range of possibilities available to you.

If you seek to grow and develop, you must treat your fund of knowledge as a living organism and continue to feed it.

You should not think of learning as something done only in the classroom. Some things are best learned in an academic or formal training setting, but most of what you learn is from outside the classroom. Knowledge grows through five modes of feeding—experiences, observations, research, communication, and contemplation.

Experience is the fundamental mode for gaining knowledge. Every moment of your life is an experience from which you can learn. From the time that you took your first breath, you have exposed yourself to learning. The exposure alone, however, does not result in increased knowledge. Knowledge is gained when you engage your mind in the experience. Think, remember, and imagine. Your actions and reactions to the situation are vital to your living knowledge. To broaden your knowledge, you must broaden your experiences.

Observation is the mode of feeding the mind with the facts and figures that are the raw material for your thoughts and beliefs. In whatever setting you find yourself, you can use your five senses—seeing, hearing, feeling, smelling, and tasting—to observe your surroundings. By observing the actions and reactions of others in various situations, you can learn much about yourself. There are unfortunate experiences you can avoid by learning from the experiences of others.

If the information you need or desire is not readily at hand, you can search and research for it. When facts, figures, and concepts are hidden, you must be able to dig deeper. Be curious. Ask questions.

It is not necessary to reinvent the wheel. If someone else has gathered facts or developed ideas, he or she can communicate them to you. Through discussions with others, academic instruction, reading books, or other forms of transmitting information, you can lengthen your reach for knowledge.

Taking in information through experience, observation, research, or communication from another, will not result in living knowledge unless you digest it all through contemplation. Through contemplation you develop ideas, establish beliefs, and inspire creativity.

Your capacity for knowledge is determined more by your attitude toward learning rather than your aptitude for learning. Your attitude toward learning is revealed in your curiosity and willingness to ask questions, your open-mindedness to a viewpoint different from your own, and your ability to listen in search for a new idea or a better idea. Limiting your intake of information to only that which you are familiar and with which you agree will stunt the growth of your body of knowledge.

You are responsible for your learning. If you contract it out, you cannot be certain that what you get will be nutrient-rich—that is, vital to a moving and growing body of truth. Contracting out is the result of accepting what you hear without questioning and verifying it. When you contract out learning, you leave yourself vulnerable to duping and manipulation. You can avoid these detriments by asking: Is it meaningful to me? Is it fact or opinion? Is there missing information? Is there another side? Is the source reliable? Is it consistent with what I know and/or have experienced?

Knowledge should not be obtained merely for the sake of having knowledge. It is not living knowledge if you hold it as a possession. The value of living knowledge increases when it is redistributed. When it is shared, living knowledge expresses the second facet—that is, contributing to meaningful living.

CHAPTER 11
USING WHAT YOU KNOW

The more knowledge you have about what you seek in life,
the greater control you have over obtaining it.

During the mid-1980's, I often played the then popular board game, Trivial Pursuit. I enjoyed the game as much as I enjoyed taking tests at school. Don't go back to read that last sentence. You read it right. I enjoyed taking tests. I appreciated challenges to my knowledge as a test to see what I had yet to learn.

Trivial Pursuit Genus Edition tested my knowledge in six categories—geography, history, entertainment, science and nature, sports and leisure, and art and literature. Starting at the hub of a six-spoke wheel, each player moves 1 to 6 spaces corresponding to the roll of a single die. He is required to answer a question in the category corresponding to the color of the space on which he lands—blue for geography, yellow for history, pink for entertainment, green for science and nature, orange for sports and leisure, and brown for art and literature. One question in each of the six categories is on each of a collection of 1,000 cards. The player's turn continues as long as he answers the question correctly. He continues to move along the circumference of the wheel or up and down the spokes trying to land on a category headquarter, which are located at the end of each spoke. When a player correctly answers the question given while on a category headquarter, he earns a wedge of the color of that category. After a player earns all six wedges to fill his game token, he attempts to return to the hub. When he lands in the hub, his opponents get to choose the category for the final question. The game is over when a player correctly answers the question after returning to the hub with all six wedges.

Jaci, her mother Juliamae, and I would get together on a weekend afternoon or evening, each setting out to be the first to get six wedges and be the first to get back to the hub. My weakness was the Art and Literature category of questions, and both Jaci and her mother sought to exploit my weakness. You could bet that when they had the chance to choose a category for me, they would choose Art and Literature.

Once, Jaci and I played Trivial Pursuit with another couple. For the sake of disguising their identity, I'll call them Rick and Rachel. We didn't follow the sage advice to split couples when forming teams to avoid one couple being the winner and the other, the loser. When you split couples, you have both a winner and a loser in each family. However, we played Dana and Jaci against Rick and Rachel.

To earn the wedge for the category of Art and Literature, which would give our team the win, I got a question the answer to which I didn't know. As I racked my brain to come up with a guess that would have a chance to be right, Rick taunted, "Oh, you don't know that?" The increased pressure did not help. I gave an answer that was incorrect.

Later on in the game, Rick got a question out of Sports and Leisure asking for the ingredients for the drink Mimosa. He didn't know the answer. I wanted so much to mimic, "Oh, you don't know that?" but I resisted and held my tongue. I again resisted the compulsion to do so when Rick didn't know what a philatelist did.

I learned from Jaci after we were married that a mimosa is made with orange juice and champagne. I came to know that a philatelist collected stamps from playing Trivial Pursuit with Jaci and Juliamae. So I managed to live, complete college and law school, and get a job as a judge without knowing how to make a mimosa or the meaning of the term philatelist. Knowing the latter two pieces of trivia might get me a win in a board game but is otherwise trivial to my career pursuit.

Toward what use do you put your knowledge?

Knowledge contributes to a meaningful life when it is useful toward getting what you want. It is living knowledge.

To make living meaningful, here are some useful things to know:

Know what you want. Knowing what you want is solidified and becomes most useful when you take the time to make a list of your needs and desires. You gain this knowledge through contemplation and self-examination. (See Chapter 31 on "Knowing What You Want" to read about making a list of your wants.)

Know why you want it. The meaningfulness of what you get lies in knowing why you want it. It is certainly possible for you to get what you want without knowing why you want it, but you will not be able to place what you get in the larger scheme of significance without knowing the basis for your desires. You can gain this knowledge through contemplation. (See Chapter 32 on "Knowing Why You Want It.")

Know where it is. To get what you want, you must know where it is. You can gain this knowledge through research. Knowing the location of what you want will help you determine where you need to be to get it. Is it tangible and movable? If so, you can stay where you are and work toward bringing it to you. Otherwise, you may have to go where it is. If you are not willing or ready to move, you might have to delete the item from your want list or postpone your getting it until you are ready to move.

Know who has it. To get what you want, you must know who has it and whether they are willing to let it go. If your desire is for something that is offered in the marketplace, of course, the owner will let it go for a price. The only issue is your willingness to pay. If, on the other hand, you are looking for an intangible such as recognition, honor, acceptance, or fame, you must gain it from those whom you have identified as the people of significance for such intangibles. Because it is often difficult to learn who holds or is responsible for giving the intangibles that you seek, gaining this knowledge will require that you search, research, and communicate with others.

You no doubt have heard it said that it is who you know, not what you know, that is important. This may be true if what you want is scarce, is the subject of much competition, and is in the control of someone else. Check your wants list again and see if fulfilling your desires will depend on who you know. Otherwise, what you know may be more useful.

Know if and when it is available. To get what you want, you must know when it is available. Some things are time sensitive—that is, there are only certain stages of your life during which they can be done. Rearing your children is one example. Your son or daughter will have only one childhood; so to have parental influence during his or her early development, you will have only one chance. Knowing when an opportunity will be available helps you to plan and prioritize your desires.

Know what it takes to get it. To get what you want, you must know how to get it. Know what costs, time, steps, and abilities are required. It is important that you know and follow the procedures, rules, and/or customs for getting something for which processes, rules, and customs have been established. You may be able to obtain something without following the rules and procedures, but that would be to leave things to chance. If you are interested in getting what you want through chance, you need know nothing. You can just sit and wait to see if it will occur. (See Chapter 33 on "Getting What You Want.")

The more knowledge you have about what you seek in life, the greater control you have over obtaining it. Just for the fun of it, you may increase your knowledge of information that is not directly useful for your getting what you want out of life, but it would be no trivial matter if you do so to the exclusion of what is meaningful to living.

Knowledge that is not used is abused.
                    - Cree Proverb

PART III:
ESTABLISHING AND NURTURING
CONNECTION

Clapping with the right hand only will not produce a noise.
                                                    - Malayan Proverb

CHAPTER 12
MEANINGFULNESS: CONNECTION

Every connection you establish—at home, at work, with your religious group, in the community, or just in passing—will be counted in the measure of the meaningfulness of your life.

I was present at the birth of my four children—Dana, Winter, Anton, and Linnea. Jaci was there too, but you'd probably figure that one out without my telling you.

We prepared for the birth of our first child. Jaci and I attended Lamaze classes and learned about the techniques of natural childbirth. We practiced breathing. I listened carefully to the instructions about measuring time between contractions. I wanted to be certain to know precisely when it was time to get to the hospital.

On Tuesday, August 28, Jaci started feeling contractions. Initially they occurred at thirty-minute intervals. When the contractions got to a frequency of every four minutes, we left home. At the hospital the doctor measured Jaci's dilation and reported that it was not enough. He invited us to walk around the hospital to encourage a larger opening. We walked...and walked...and walked. Jaci rested and we walked some more. About eighteen hours later, at 4:47 P.M. on August 29, 1984, our first son was born.

Our second child, Winter, did not require Jaci's walking to promote dilation. It might have, but I refused to stay at the hospital on our first trip. We went to the hospital in early November 1985 when we thought Jaci's contractions were close enough together to warrant such. When we arrived, again the doctor suggested that we could walk. I said, "Hell no! We'll go home and come back when the water breaks."

We went home. We celebrated Thanksgiving expecting that any moment the baby would be born. Jaci's mother joined us for Thanksgiving, hoping that her second grandchild would enter the world while Nana was visiting California. On December 2, the Monday following the Thanksgiving weekend, Winter was born. Nana had returned to Brooklyn, and I had gone back to work. Jaci called me about an hour after my workday began to report that her water broke. With my assistant, who was also a long-time friend, driving as fast as the law would allow—maybe a little faster—I got home. My parents met me there to stay with Dana, who was then only fifteen months old. My assistant then rushed Jaci and me to the hospital. Our first daughter was born about an hour after we arrived.

An hour after arrival to the hospital would have been great for the birth of our third child and second son, but Anton would have nothing of it. Jaci woke me up about 3:30 in the morning to tell me that she was having contractions.

"How far apart are they?" I asked.

"Ten minutes," Jaci reported.

I immediately picked up the telephone to call Jaci's mother, who by then lived two doors away from us in Lancaster, California. She would have to drive us to Antelope Valley Hospital because my driving wouldn't get us there. Juliamae didn't grasp the immediacy of the situation. She told me that she would put on some clothes and make herself some coffee. The trip from home to the hospital was three miles. We got there at 5:35 in the morning. Anton was born at 5:46 on Tuesday, May 17.

We made the same trip from home to the hospital for Linnea on Monday, August 12. It was in plenty of time. Time enough to check in, for the nurses to set everything up, including helping me to put on my scrubs. At 1:32 P.M., our fourth child and second daughter was born.

While the circumstances of their births were different, there was one thing common to the entry into this world of all four of my children—they came empty-handed. They brought nothing but themselves.

What did you bring into this world?

You came into this world with nothing tangible. You had no clothes, no food, no money, and no place to live except where someone was willing to take you in. You were completely dependent on the Good Will of the universe. The Good Will of the universe was willing to sustain you for the treasures you held within, not for anything tangible that you could give; you had nothing tangible to give. What you brought to contribute to this world were your unique talents, ability to create ideas, and capacity to love. With these intangible assets you connect with the world. Your thoughts, feelings, and actions shape the world you inhabit. The universe needs your talent, your ideas, and your love to maintain Good Will.

The only way for you to share your unique intangible gifts is through connection with others. When you display your talents, somebody sees them. When you share your ideas, someone else considers them. When you love, another person receives and is nourished by your love. There is no value in your talent or your ideas or your love if they do not connect with a recipient. Consequently, you reveal the value of your existence and what you have to contribute to the world by establishing relationships—as many relationships as you can. The more that you share with others, the more meaning there is in your living.

When you came into this world, you came into a setting with billions of people and, therefore, billions of opportunities to connect and share your gifts. Your intangible gifts have no limit. With such endless resource you never have to worry about running out...about not having enough. You can share your talent without diminishing it. In fact, when you share it, you augment it. You can share your ideas without losing them. One idea is just the precursor to another, so sharing one will make room for others. You can love without diminishing the power of your love. Love is strengthened as love is given.

Just as when you came into this world you brought nothing tangible, you will leave this world taking nothing with you. You will leave behind your house and all its furnishings; you will leave your cars, no matter how many of them you have; you will leave all your credit cards and investment portfolios. You will not take with you your Android, iPhone, or Blackberry. No matter how much you accumulate while you are here, it all stays behind.

What also stays behind is the impact that your intangible gifts have on the lives of the people with whom you connect. The enormity of your impact will be determined person to person, not by the size of your audience at any given time. Every connection you establish—at home, at work, with your religious group, in the community, or just in passing—will be counted in the measure of the meaningfulness of your life.

The executor of your will or the administrator of your estate (if you don't write a will) will determine the monetary value of the things you leave behind and will distribute them as you or the law specifies. However, you alone are the administrator of the intangible assets that you possess. While you live, you determine the value of your thoughts, emotions, and actions and with whom they should be shared. You have to establish relationships and connect with your environment now. You will not be able to do it through a will after you're gone.

CHAPTER 13
DEVELOPING RELATIONSHIPS

It is within your power to ensure that the time you spend with others is time well spent.

My blindness is somewhat of an obstacle when it comes to initiating new relationships. Only in a few situations can I be the person who starts the conversation. Generally, I don't know that the person is there until he or she speaks up first.

This relationship handicap was particularly pronounced when I left home just before my eighteenth birthday to go to Yale. The only person I knew at Yale was my high-school friend, Harvey. He was a year ahead of me. We met when both of us were members of the tutoring club, which was part of the California Scholarship Federation. Harvey had been accepted at Yale in his senior year and encouraged me, then a junior, to apply.

On my first trip to Yale in September 1970, Harvey and I flew together from Los Angeles to New York and then took Connecticut Limousine from JFK Airport to New Haven. Harvey was with me when I entered Phelps Gate, and found my room, 166 in Lawrence Hall, on Old Campus. I met my roommates David and Harry; then Harvey was off to do his thing. I saw Harvey a couple of times within the first two days of my being on campus, and then didn't see him again for a month. We rarely had contact on campus thereafter. Without an effort on the part of the two individuals, the paths of a college freshman and that of a college sophomore would seldom intersect.

David and Harry became my points of contact with the rest of my college mates in my early weeks of orientation on the Yale campus. One of them would accompany me to the Commons for meals. One of them—usually David— would walk with me till I learned how to get to my classes on my own. David took me to the laundry room in the basement of Berkeley, our residential hall.

I met fellow students in the dining hall and in the classroom. I also met other students when I sat outside on a bench on Old Campus taking in the sun and the fresh air. They would come and sit—or stand—and initiate a conversation. "I've seen you walking across the campus" or "I'm in your calculus class" might be the way someone would start a conversation after introducing him- or herself. Besides the usual questions about where I'm from and what other classes I'm taking, I got questions about how I manage to get around the campus on my own, how I kept up with all the reading, and how I did my work to turn it in to the professors. The conversation often ended with the exchange of phone numbers and an offer from my new acquaintance to read whenever I needed someone to do so.

I met Debbie Katz one day while sitting out on the campus. She introduced herself and told me that she was in the same anthropology class with me. Since the class met at one o'clock in the afternoon, Debbie suggested that we have lunch together in Commons just before class the next day. I always jumped at the chance to have someone accompany me to the dining hall. It was difficult to impossible for me to navigate the dining hall with a cane in the right hand and a food tray in the left.

The next day, Debbie and I met as planned. We walked together from Lawrence Hall on Old Campus a couple of blocks to Commons. We went through the cafeteria line with Debbie explaining my choices for lunch and putting the dishes I selected on my tray. Moving from left to right we got to the end of the line with Debbie on my left. Then I heard an unfamiliar voice coming from my right.

"Hi, my name is Pat. Would you have lunch with me?"

While I tried to explain that I was having lunch with my friend, Debbie, Pat grabbed my tray, pushed her left elbow into my right hand, and said, "Debbie can have lunch with us, too."

We reached a table that was already filled with guests. Pat introduced me to five guys. I only remember that two of them were named Mike. None of them stated their names. Pat called out their names without indicating where they were sitting, so I don't consider myself to have met them. None of them talked to me during lunch. They all talked to Pat, trying their best to get her phone number because she, a sophomore, was the rare student who lived off campus in her own apartment and had her own car. I remained mostly silent and feeling quite awkward during the meal. I didn't know where Debbie was. I didn't even know if she had followed us to the table. It turned out that she was right across the table from me. She no doubt felt as awkward as I did. I answered the occasional question that Pat asked. Debbie finally spoke up and said we had better get going to class so as not to be late. It was only then that I knew she was right across the table from me.

As Debbie and I got up to leave, Pat said, "Dana, let me give you my telephone number. Call me some time."

My feeling of embarrassment vanished immediately. These five guys at the table had not been successful in getting Pat's telephone number even though they repeatedly asked for it, and here she was offering it to me and I didn't ask.

During my first visit to Pat's apartment to have dinner, she explained to me why she initiated our having lunch together. She explained that when I entered Commons with Debbie, one of the guys said, "I feel sorry for the brother. Every time I see him he is with a white girl."

Pat suggested, "That's probably because none of you black students ever go up to talk to him."

One of the guys retorted, "I would if I had the chance."

Pat told me that she got up immediately and said, "I'm going to give you your chance." She then got me from the cafeteria line and took me to the table where they were sitting.

Pat Lambright and I developed a great college relationship. She invited me to her parents' home in Queens for Thanksgiving. She often drove me to New York to visit my cousins in the Bronx when she was going home for the weekend. We continued to exchange Christmas cards about twenty-five years after graduating from college.

What relationships are you cultivating?

Unless you have taken a vow of solitude, in your day-to-day activities you are involved in relationships with other people—relationships of all degrees of significance.

You may be accustomed to thinking of relationships as those personal interactions you have affirmatively created with some intent of intimacy and/or duration. However, every interaction with another person, no matter how brief or distant the encounter might be, is a relationship. Every interaction you have with another person is an event that takes time; that is, each relationship that you have with a family member, friend, coworker, passing acquaintance, or other person involves a sharing of part of your life. It is within your power to ensure that the time you spend with others is time well spent. You determine if the time is meaningful. If the time you spend with Zeke, Chantice, Carmen, or Nguyen is meaningful, then the relationship with him or her is meaningful.

The first step to determining the meaningfulness of your relationship with another person is to identify the point of common interest. The point of common interest is the factor that brings two people together. It is the explanation of how you came to meet or to know the person. Below is a list of eleven ways to label your day-to-day interactions based on the point of common interest.

Family—wife, husband, life partner, children, grandchildren, brother, sister, parent, grandparent, aunt, uncle, cousins, and so on. The point of common interest is genetic (or blood) and can also be by law. Your family by law can be by marriage or by adoption. Notwithstanding the fact that you can choose to bear children, your biological family relationships are without choice. You don't get to choose whether you will have a son or a daughter. You don't get to pick your parents, sisters, brothers, and so forth. You can choose your spousal partner, but the stepchildren and the in-laws come with the package. You can also choose the child that you foster or adopt. Your interactions with your family may be out of a sense of moral obligation—the obligation that comes with family ties.

Neighbor—the person who lives in geographic proximity to you. The point of common interest is a particular mass of land. Except when you first move in to your current residence, rarely, if ever, do you get to choose who your neighbors will be. You can, however, choose whether or not to be neighborly.

Coworker or Colleague—the people who are hired by the employer who hired you. The point of common interest is the job. You may refer to your coworker as a colleague if you have similar professional skills. As with neighbors, you don't usually get to choose the people with whom you will work. There are two exceptions. When you first make your employment decision, you are deciding on your coworkers; when you have the authority to hire new employees, you get to choose coworkers. The extent of your relationship with your coworker is limited by the time clock, the calendar, and your work assignment. Even if you work closely with a fellow employee, your relationship with her begins at starting time and ends at quitting time. You have no connection with her on your days off.

Associate—a person you work with but who is not hired by your employer. The point of common interest is a particular project or assignment of your job. Your relationship with them exists only to the point of completing a particular project or assignment. When the dealings are done, the relationship ends.

Beneficiary—customers, patrons, clients, consumers. The point of common interest is the service or product that you provide as part of your job assignment. The extent of your relationship is based on the completion of the service or transaction.

Competitor—a person vying for the same beneficiaries whom you seek. The point of common interest is the same or similar business. These are relationships that you would doubtless choose not to have since they involve interaction with people who are working against your goals and/or best interest. It is noted here that two athletes on opposing teams are not competitors in the sense discussed here because they are serving the same customer and not working against each other to serve that customer. The two athletes are associates.

Consumer—when you are the beneficiary, or potential beneficiary, of a product or service. The point of common interest is the business or marketing transaction. If you answered the telephone call of a solicitor or you transacted business with a store clerk, you experienced a consumer relationship. You have probably sought to block the calls of telephone marketers because you do not wish to have a relationship with them. As to the personnel working in the businesses that you patronize, they are not relationships that you seek out. It is the business transaction that motivates your patronage. Nevertheless, the consumer relationship occurs.

Cohort—a person who is a member in the organization that you belong to. The point of common interest is your group membership. The group can be an organization such as Lions, Delta Sigma Theta, school PTA, or your church. If you are not the one who gets to choose who joins the group, you have no choice in who your cohorts will be. Nevertheless, you interact with them because they have joined the same organization to which you belong.

Incidental relationship—one that occurs incidental to another. The point of common interest is another person. One incidental relationship might be interaction with your coworker's husband because he joined his wife at an office party. Another could be with the son of a cohort whose telephone call you returned and you talked with the son because his dad was not at home.

Socializer—a person you meet at a social event. The point of common interest is the event itself. By chance, the two of you ended up at the same movie theater, the same bar, or the same fundraising dinner.

Passing acquaintance—met only in passing through. These are relationships that are formed when you sit next to each other on the plane, ride the commuter train to work, or talk in the waiting room at the dentist's office. The point of common interest is the chance of your being in the same place at the same time. A relationship as a passing acquaintance is also formed when you assist a blind woman across a busy intersection.

If your relationship with another person never develops to be more than just the point of common interest, then the contribution that relationship gives to your living a meaningful life rests wholly on the meaningfulness of the common interest. For example, if your work does not satisfy your yearning to make a difference in this world, then your relationships with coworkers will not either. The portion of your life that you spend doing a meaningless job will also be spent in relationships that offer no significance to living. In your quest to make each moment meaningful then, you must seek to do two things regarding your relationships with others. First, you must make sure that your interests—that is, the things you devote your life to—are related to meaningfulness. They must fulfill your purpose, promote your growth, and/or help to define your thoughts, emotions, principles, and beliefs. The second thing to do is to cultivate your relationships to develop beyond a point of common interest. If a relationship never evolves beyond the point of common interest, that other person cannot be relied on to be a partner in your efforts to make each moment of your life meaningful.

CHAPTER 14
MAKING FRIENDS

*If you can't take your friends with you everywhere you go,
make friends wherever you are.*

Peter and I became friends through our membership in Toastmasters International. We were not in the same Toastmasters club when we met. In fact, we were not in the same district. Living in San Pedro, California, Peter was in Toastmasters' District 1; I was in District 33.

In the spring of 1993, I was invited to be a guest speaker at the semi-annual conference of District 1 Toastmasters, a district that included the City of Los Angeles (below the Santa Monica Freeway) and the adjacent cities to the south. At the conference, I met a member who organized groups of Toastmasters to visit Terminal Island Federal Correctional Institution to hold Toastmasters meetings for the inmates. I agreed to participate, and on my first visit I met Peter.

Before driving back to Lancaster from San Pedro, Jaci and I joined Peter and his friend for dinner after the Toastmasters meeting. From the dinner conversation, I learned of Peter's goal to participate in the World Championship of Public Speaking. I had recently won the competition and offered to provide him support and coaching.

Peter entered the International Speech Contest in the spring of 1996, having joined the same club of which I was a member. The district level competition, the fourth of six levels, was held in Ventura, California. I sat in the audience and enjoyed Peter's speech in which he shared stories about his work as a doctor in an emergency room and the connection his work gave him to serving people. In the post-contest interviews, Peter told the audience that he wanted one day to work with an organization of medical professionals known as Doctors Without Borders. When Peter returned to the table of his local cheering section, I quizzed him as to what was stopping him from joining Doctors Without Borders immediately. I offered that as a single man with no children, there seemed to be no reason for him to wait. If he simply made the decision to do it, he could work with Doctors Without Borders soon. He did. He got past his excuses for postponing his dream and worked out the details of making it happen.

As we continued our relationship, Peter reciprocated encouragement and support to me. His financial support helped me to complete my first book, which was published in 1997.

Who do you hold as a friend?

To have a friend is the most significant relationship you can hold. Friend is greater than family because family only describes a point of common interest. In friendship you have both a point of common interest and a promise of mutual benefit. Of course, when a family member is your friend, you have the ultimate relationship.

Friendship is always a matter of choice. You choose the person with whom you want to be a friend. You choose the benefits you are willing to give and those you believe you can obtain from your friend. You choose how close you want to hold a friend.

The first step to determining the meaningfulness of a relationship is the point of common interest. (See Chapter 13 on "Developing Relationships.") The second step to determining the meaningfulness of your relationship with another person is to identify the promise of mutual benefit. The combination of a point of common interest and a promise of mutual benefit is the bond that creates a friend.

The "promise" of "promise of benefit" is a key element because it denotes both a basis for expectation and a commitment to do something. As you assess the people that you meet in whatever context, you must look for what benefit they can offer to your living meaningfully and their willingness to share that benefit with you. Be careful not to confuse benefit with money. In your quest to making the moment meaningful as it concerns relationships, you will learn that the greatest benefits are those on which you cannot put a price. Here are six ways a benefit might come to you:

A benefit can be physical. You may need a person to be nearby because you are afraid to be alone or because you cannot be left alone. You may need a person to help you do something because you don't have the strength, skill, capacity or time to do it yourself or by yourself. You may desire person-to-person contact—to hold hands, to hug, to kiss. You may want sexual stimulation and gratification.

A benefit can be mental. You can expand your knowledge by learning from someone else—a teacher, a tutor, a mentor. Your creativity can be ignited when someone else shares his or her ideas with you. Your beliefs can be shaped and your principles formed through conversation, discussions, or debates with others.

A benefit can be emotional. Love is always a benefit whether it is expressed as care, concern, devotion, empathy, or sympathy. At the time when you are feeling down, you can benefit from something said or something done that lifts your spirit or encourages you to move on.

A benefit can be spiritual. Someone can pray for you. Someone can guide you to enlightenment. You can commune spirit to spirit with another soul.

A benefit can be social. Having a partner with whom you can play sports and games is a benefit. Having a partner with whom you can watch television, go to the movies, or attend a concert is a benefit. Having a partner with whom you can walk around the block or along the beach is a benefit.

A benefit can be financial. There is clearly a benefit when someone meets your need for food, shelter, clothing, transportation, and/or health care; pays your bills; funds your education or business; gives you a job, or gives you any tangible possession.

A friendship is never one-sided. If you assess in another person a promise of benefit, you must also offer a promise of benefit. If the other person does not get a benefit from having a relationship with you, the relationship cannot be meaningful to her or him.

Don't confuse mutuality with equality. The benefits that you exchange in a friendship need not be the same. To use the categories mentioned above, they need not come the same way. You might get the emotional benefit of encouragement from another person; your benefit to him might be physical—a walking partner. You might provide the motivation for another person who builds a successful business—an emotional benefit; she in turn gives you a job—a financial benefit. It is not a meaningful relationship if you must take out a calculator or some other measurement scale to see if you've gotten equality in monetary value.

A friend can be a family member, a neighbor, a coworker or colleague, an associate, or a cohort. The relationship formed as a point of common interest need not change in order for a friendship to develop. On the other hand, if you develop a friendship from a relationship that formed as incidental, socializer, or passing acquaintance, the original characterization of the relationship disappears. In other words, a friendship cannot be incidental, mere socializer, or passing acquaintance. Beneficiary, consumer, and competitor relationships may evolve into friendships, but the transformation can involve ethical concerns.

The degree of closeness in your friendships depends on three factors—longevity, trust, and love. The numbers of years that you have been friends with someone can determine the intimacy of the relationship because of the time you have had to get to know each others thoughts, feelings, desires, and dreams. Because of the longevity, you can survive the stresses that visit personal relationships and stick together even when there are momentary disagreements. Even if a friendship has not had the test of time, the closeness between friends can be measured by the extent to which they trust each other. You can trust a close friend with your personal information; secrets; foibles, failings, and flaws; and vulnerabilities without concern that your friend will share the knowledge with someone else or take advantage of your weaknesses. However, the ultimate test of the closeness of your friendship is love. When you can freely and without hesitation use the word love to describe your emotional connection with your friend, you demonstrate that your friendship is close—close to oneness. By the same token, if you are more comfortable with words such as care, concern, fond, and like, you indicate the degree to which you see your friendship.

Since every encounter or interaction you have with another person involves sharing a part of your life, you should seek to spend as much time as you can with friends. That is, you should spend every moment possible with persons with whom you choose to have a relationship, with whom you have a common interest, from whom you gain a meaningful benefit and to whom you want to give a benefit, and with whom you can share a degree of emotional intimacy. How meaningful would life be for you if you lived with friends, went to work with friends, had business transactions with friends, played with friends, and worshipped with friends? If you can't take your friends with you everywhere you go, make friends wherever you are. Friendships don't just happen. They don't form spontaneously. The establishment of a friend requires action on your part. You must be friendly.

If you spend time on a relationship from which you gain no benefit, you are not willing to give a benefit, and there is no degree of emotional intimacy, you are in a detractor relationship. A detractor consumes your life and adds nothing toward your living meaningfully. As vigorously as you seek to form friendships, you must avoid detractors.

CHAPTER 15
NURTURING BENEFICIAL RELATIONSHIPS

*The life you were intended to live is enriched and made
meaningful according to the relationships that you develop
and nurture.*

In all stages of my life—those stages of education,
employment, church, and general growth and maturity—I
developed relationships which today I do not maintain. At
McKinley Elementary School, Michael and I were the best of
friends; I have not heard from or seen him since about 1965. I
was chummy with Karen, Bill, and Caroline, among others,
in junior high school, but I haven't seen any of these three in
forty years. I have no regular contact with any of the other
blind students who attended John Marshall High School with
me. The group of about eighteen of us were rather close in
high school because of our common needs and because we
rode the school bus together for trips lasting more than an
hour. In the sixties and seventies at Trinity Chapel, if you
saw me, you saw Frank, Melvin, and/or Vincent. I no longer
am a member of that church and have not had contact with
those three guys in more than twenty years.

My relationships with Michael, Bill, Karen, Caroline,
Frank, Melvin, Vincent, and the other blind students in high
school did not have unfriendly ends. We grew out of them,
and our lives diverged to directions which made the
relationships no longer beneficial. Nevertheless, the person
that I am today was influenced by those relationships.

There are some friendships that I formed in my teen-age
years that have remained till now. I met Seebee at church in
the sixties; we are still friends. In the course of time our
relationship has evolved and changed to fit our interests.
Initially we were friends at church. Then I hired her to work

as my secretary at the Disabled Resources Center. A couple of years after I left DRC, she became an assistant to read and drive for me when I worked for the State of California. She stopped working for me in 1986, but we have maintained our friendship through telephone conversations three or four times a year.

Harvey, whom I have mentioned elsewhere in this book, and Vykee are friends that I gained while at John Marshall High School. Today we are still friends, but the nature of our friendship has changed, owing to the different directions our lives have taken. The friendship I have with each is nourished with not much more than telephone contacts a few times a year and face-to-face interactions about once every five years.

Emily, Marciana, and I were such tight friends at Marshall High School that I would have sworn we'd be such friends for the rest of our lives. However, I lost all contact with them both after 1980. Recently our connection with each other was reestablished. Emily sent me an e-mail message in early 2010 after finding me through an internet search. Marciana found me on Facebook in 2011. We got together when Marciana visited Southern California from her home in Nashville, Tennessee. Over a restaurant dinner, Emily, Marciana, and I, along with Naomi, another classmate, reminisced of our high-school days for four hours. The strength of our relationships established at Marshall permitted the reunion more than thirty years later.

Why do we establish and maintain the relationships that we do?

We were made to be social creatures. The life you were intended to live is enriched and made meaningful according to the relationships that you develop and nurture.

The relationship that you have with another person exists as a thought in your mind about the connection that the two of you have. Maybe you will share your thoughts with him or her, and maybe you won't. Often you will operate under assumptions without conversation about the nature of your relationship with another person. Rarely are the terms of a relationship put in writing. It may happen in a business dealing. A marital relationship is confirmed in writing for recognition in law as to the establishment of the relationship, but the terms and conditions of the relationship may not be written at all, except in instances where prenuptial agreements are established concerning property matters.

Difficulties will arise in a relationship when the thoughts that you have about your connection with another do not match the thoughts she or he has about connection with you. For example, you may believe that Eric is your friend. Operating under a different belief, Eric does something to you that is not at all indicative of friendship. His snubbing you might prompt you to say, "I thought he was my friend." Your thought may have been correct. The problem is that Eric's thought about his relationship with you was not the same as yours.

You nurture beneficial relationships when you say and do things that ensure that your thoughts about the relationship agree with the thoughts the other person has toward the relationship. Through your words and actions, you can clarify misunderstanding and confirm expectations. Nurturing involves communicating, listening, sharing, giving, and forgiving.

Nurturing is communicating, not just thinking. Thoughts alone do not create relationships, and thoughts alone cannot strengthen them. You must communicate your thoughts to the relationship partner. You can talk on the phone, visit his or her home, meet for lunch, or converse at a social function. If face-to-face conversation is difficult or not possible, you can send a letter, card, email, or text message. Your actions can serve to communicate your thoughts, but actions are subject to interpretation, and your actions may not be interpreted by the relationship partner the way you intended. You can avoid misinterpretation by accompanying your actions with words that communicate your intended message. For example, you might invite a friend to share an apartment as a way to reduce your monthly living expenses, and he may interpret the offer as an invitation to establish a conjugal relationship. By discussing the offer with each other, you can be sure that the two of you are thinking the same thing about the invitation.

A relationship that is completely devoid of communication will eventually, if not more immediately, fade away as do all other thoughts that are not expressed.

Nurturing involves listening, not just talking. Mutually beneficial relationships require two-way communication for sustenance. You have to be a listener when your relationship partner is communicating. Listen in patient silence. Encourage your partner's communication by showing interest and curiosity. Ask questions when the message you hear is not clear.

If you are not willing to listen, you can't reasonably expect your partner to be a listener either. If no one is listening, there is no communicating.

Nurturing involves sharing interests, ideas, and aspirations, not just doing things together. Your friendship began with the sharing of a common interest, and a common interest is required to maintain the relationship. The nature of the interest may change, but there must still be a shared interest. You may have met as coworkers and developed a friendship that has survived notwithstanding the fact you no longer work together. Saturday morning golfing now might be the common interest of your relationship. The ultimate in sharing is a common interest in fulfilling your purpose. The best relationship to cultivate is with one who provides you a benefit that is consistent with your fulfilling your purpose while you likewise provide your friend a benefit toward fulfillment of his or her purpose.

It is possible for you to become so busy with what you are doing that you neglect the relationships with the people with whom you are doing it. You can, for example, be preoccupied with making a living and neglect and eventually lose the partner for whom you were making a living.

If there is nothing more for you and your friend or partner to share, there is no basis for maintaining the relationship.

Nurturing involves giving, not just getting. There is no reason for you to maintain and nurture a relationship from which you derive no benefit. If you get no benefit, the time you devote to the relationship is wasted life. It doesn't matter what the point of common interest is—family, coworker, cohort, consumer, etc. To be worth your time and effort to maintain, you must get a benefit.

Everything I just wrote in the previous paragraph applies to your relationship partner as well. That is, she or he must derive a benefit from the relationship; otherwise, to expend energy and time to maintain the relationship with you would be a waste of her or his life. You must give as readily and willingly as you receive. If in your friendship each of you focuses on the giving of benefits, both of you will receive.

When an individual has identified a benefit that she needs, she will pursue it. If she can't get it from having a friendship with you, she'll establish a friendship with someone else.

The benefit that you gain from a relationship must itself be meaningful. In other words, the benefit must promote your growth and development, help you to fulfill your purpose, and not violate your guiding principles. If your relationship with another person does not meet these meaningfulness standards, then the relationship can't be considered to be meaningful even if there is a give-and-take involved.

Nurturing involves forgiving, not just forgetting. You have feelings and are subject to being hurt. Your relationship partner likewise has feelings and can be hurt. The closer you become connected, the greater the likelihood that one of you will offend the other. Your strength, courage, and willingness to forgive will prolong your friendship. It is not healthy for the relationship for you to simply sweep the matter under the rug. Eventually the pile of dirt and trash will be evident even if you think it is covered up. To get rid of the offense that might permanently damage the relationship, you must talk, listen, forgive, learn from, and forget. In this context, forgetting does not mean to wipe it clean from your memory. It means to release it so it does not become the seed of grudge or resurfacing of blame.

If you are unable to forgive a person for an offense toward you, your relationship with that person is doomed to fail. A wound that is allowed to fester and not heal will jeopardize the health of a friendship.

Mutually beneficial relationships require altruism for nurturing and sustenance. Altruism is the unselfish interest in the well-being of others. To maintain a meaningful relationship, you must be able to place the well-being of the other person on the same level of priority as your own. If your friend, relative, spouse, partner, or colleague perceives that you approach the relationship with a me-first attitude, he or she will adopt a similar attitude toward the relationship and hold back on his or her commitment to you. If, with your me-first approach to things, you perceive a diminished interest in the relationship, you will likely act even more with a what's-in-it-for-me attitude. Eventually, this spiraling down in the relationship will lead to an end to the relationship or, at best, to a connection of merely convenience or obligation. Acting altruistically, on the other hand, strengthens your relationship ties and with both of you working toward the benefit of each other. In a mutually beneficial altruistic relationship, neither partner has to sacrifice his or her desires and goals toward meaningful living; they work together to achieve the goals of both parties.

The meaningful benefit that you need to sustain a meaningful relationship may change as you grow and develop. What you needed in a friendship in elementary school, for example, is different from that needed in your friendships as a married parent. Consequently, you must be willing to establish new relationships rather than seeking to hold on to the old.

Hold a true friend with both your hands.
- Nigerian Proverb

CHAPTER 16
LETTING LOVE FLOW

The power of love may cause you to resist its full expression;
but if you resist, you also may miss its full benefit.

Even before my friend, Sharon, was pregnant, she talked excitedly about the prospect of having a baby. I asked her why she wanted so much to have a child. She said that she wanted someone to love her. I loved her, but it wasn't my love that she wanted. She had another man in mind. Sharon had a baby and married the baby's father. After a time, Sharon divorced the daddy. After a time, Sharon's baby grew up and moved to the opposite side of the country, vowing never to talk to her mother again. I am not certain Sharon ever got the love that she wanted before dying of cancer.

I left the practice of law where I handled divorces and probate matters because I was saddened by the absence of love between married couples and within families. Once two people decided that the marital relationship was over, so was love. In fact, love was replaced with anger and hate. The two people who once pledged a lifetime together switched to a commitment to destroy each other even if they hurt themselves, their children, and their property in the process.

In divorcing her husband, Beverly wanted the house, the property, the kids, and spousal and child support. She cut up her husband's clothes and broke out windows in the house. Yes, the house that she wanted.

Melanie, who was my client, thought she and Charles should share custody of their two-year-old child, but Charles thought he should have sole custody. He and his attorney would not come to an agreement with my client for joint custody until the judge threatened to award custody to both with each having physical custody on alternate days.

I witnessed the absence of love between siblings when there was the issue of how to distribute inheritance. Though the law of intestate succession in California provides for equal distribution, the oldest of Kathy's several children thought he should get a greater share of the $120,000 his mother left behind. He believed he was entitled to a greater share of the inheritance because he spent more time than did his brothers and sisters caring for their mother in her last illness.

I asked the son, "When you took care of your mother, did you expect to be paid to do so?"

"No. I took care of her because I loved her," he responded without hesitation.

"Then why now do you expect to be paid?" I followed up.

The son did not answer and did not let up on his effort to secure a bigger share of his mother's property for himself. His attitude and efforts caused a riff in the family that exists to this day. Siblings took sides and one side does not communicate with the other.

I knew Kathy pretty well and am certain that what she demonstrated to her children about love is not at all what they have displayed toward each other after her death.

What is love?

Love is the essence of your being. You were created to be a source of love and to be a vessel that receives love. Loving is as natural to the soul as eating and breathing is to the body. You did not have to be taught to eat or breathe; you did them as an instinct for survival. Your instinct for survival stems from your loving yourself. You did not have to be taught to give and receive love.

Love is connection. It is your capacity and willingness to reach out beyond yourself and connect with another person or with another element of creation. When you love, the object of your love becomes an essential part of your living.

Love is giving. If love is the motivation for everything that you do, you become a giver. The result of your actions will be to give and to serve others. You act in concert with the rest of nature, which was created to give, not to hoard. Saving and accumulating material possessions are not necessarily actions outside or in disharmony with love. They are consistent with love if they are done with love as a motivation. In other words, you can save and accumulate with the motivation to give what you have amassed for the benefit of others. If you are motivated otherwise, you become a hoarder whose sole purpose for accumulating possessions is to deprive others of what you possess.

Love is forgiving. Love is not blind to flaws, faults, and wrongs done. Love sees them, forgives them, and lets them lie in the past. Love has the capacity of cooling down anger. Love lacks the capacity to hold a grudge toward another. The forgiving characteristic of love soothes pain and promotes healing. Without love you would be motivated to put up defenses for offenses committed against you, to seek payback for pain caused you, and to return evil for evil done to you.

Love is demonstrated through action—acts of kindness, understanding, patience, and goodness. You may use words to express an emotion or a motivation, but language is inadequate to show love. Language by itself is inadequate, so words alone cannot convey love. You show love by what you do for the benefit of the person you love. Your patience and understanding reflect your willingness to be forgiving.

Love can be felt, but it is not the feeling. When you love, it may be manifested in a joyful emotion that brings warmth and causes you to smile. This emotional reaction is just a physical benefit of giving and receiving love. Love is the reason for your being what you are and doing what you do to become a part of the life of another person. That reason can be firm even if you do not feel it. In other words, love is both a matter of the heart and a matter of the mind. When you acknowledge love as the motivation for your actions, you are loving even if you are not feeling in love.

Love is formless. It takes the shape of the situation for which it is called and is expressed accordingly. In a lifetime partnership, it is the will to hold to a commitment of forever together. In a business setting, it is the attention given in serving a customer. At a funeral service for a friend, it is your presence and words of comfort. In your community, it is your volunteering to work at a soup kitchen for the homeless or hungry.

You may express love as like, affection, care, compassion, empathy, adoration, cherish, infatuation, devotion, fondness, regard, or passion. These are some of the many forms that love can take on.

Love is boundless. It has no limits as to age, gender, race, social status, geography, language, time, physical condition, or education. If you open your soul and let love flow in its natural course, you will love old and young; you will love people of all colors; you will love men and women, you will love rich and poor; you will love people living inside and outside your national borders; you will love now and later.

In the course of your experiences, whether they be positive or negative, you may develop a concept of love that permits you to decide who you will and who you will not love. Such a concept is not love because love has no restrictions. There is no spigot on your soul that allows you to turn love off and on depending on the person. If you function with such a spigot, what flows out of it is egotism, not love. Egotism permits you to focus on what's best for you. You can then feign affection for another person to get the benefit that you seek for yourself.

Love has no conditions. Conditions establish limits, and love is limitless. There can be no such thing as conditional love; hence, the term "unconditional love" is a redundancy.

Love is eternal. It can never run out because it feeds on itself. That is, the acts of giving and of forgiving enhance your ability to give and to forgive. The growth of love is accelerated when more and more people love.

If you limit your capacity or willingness to reach out to connect with another person, you interrupt the natural flow of love. You open space for the growth of fear, distrust, intolerance, anger, and malice. The more you hold back on loving, the more space there is for these destructive emotions to flourish. The heart and mind where trust and tolerance have no place are vessels of hatred. The heart and mind where fear, anger, and malice have no limit are vessels of hatred. When love is absent, hate abounds.

Love is powerful. It has the strength to hold a marriage together. It has the bond to keep a mother and her wayward child connected. It can carry two friends through periods of disagreement. Love is a force that can withstand all forces of evil and destruction.

With all the power that love possesses, love never causes pain. Pain may be caused by the absence of love. The antidote to such pain is not to thwart the flow of love. Because the forgiving characteristic of love has the power to heal, you should open your soul to love more.

The power of love may cause you to resist its full expression; but if you resist, you also miss its full benefit. Let love flow. It is not necessary for you to control its flow. Love is self-controlling. If you are willing to follow, love will lead you to your meaningfulness.

Avarice hoards itself poor; charity gives itself rich.
                                    - German Proverb

PART IV:
DISCOVERING PURPOSE

Ask questions from your heart, and you will be answered from your heart.

- Native American Proverb

CHAPTER 17
MEANINGFULNESS: PURPOSE

Threaded through one's very soul is purpose, which is woven into the design of the universe.

Having become completely blind at age four, a phrase I often heard other people say during my childhood and teen years was "He can't." I refused to accept this pronouncement of my fate. I thought, "They don't know. They don't know what I can do." The more I heard the phrase, the more I resisted the chance that I might internalize the notion and accept it as my belief. I hardened my stance. I began to think *I can.* Eventually, my I-can became I-will. I resolved that I would show them all that blindness need not stop one from doing and living. It does not diminish desire or limit ability. After mature reflection, I have come to understand that the power in I-can is the belief that I have a purpose, and, notwithstanding my blindness, I have the talents and can acquire the skills to fulfill that purpose.

Why are you here?

You have a role to play in the completeness and sustenance of the universe. Your role is no less important than the role played by the tree that provides shade. Your role is no less significant than the role the carrot plays in providing life-sustaining nutrients. The role you are to play is no less meaningful than that of the sun and the rain to promote the growth of living creation. You may be called to provide comfort, nourishment, or encouragement. The difference between you and the other elements of creation—the sun, the wind, the rain, the plants, the animals, the minerals—is that you have a choice. You get to choose whether or not you will fulfill your purpose. You get to choose the way that you will fulfill your purpose. You get to choose when you will start or stop living with purpose. You can wait until you have retired from a job before you start living with purpose, or you can choose purposefully when taking a job.

You have purpose. Threaded through your soul is purpose, which is woven into the design of the universe. You have a unique role in completing the color, texture, and beauty of life's tapestry. Because purpose is soulful, it doesn't matter the condition of the body. Men and women have purpose. Purpose is not negated by the color of your skin, the texture of your hair, the height of your frame, or the mass of your form. Notwithstanding your visual acuity, you have purpose. No matter the method of your mobility, you have purpose. Your mental functioning, expanded or restricted, does not affect purpose. Your physical and mental capacity only determine the means by which you fulfill your purpose.

When you acknowledge your purpose, it becomes the basis for your plans and goals. In the face of challenge, your purpose is the strength of determination. In a wave of despair, it is a buoy of hope. Across a chasm of insignificance, your purpose is a bridge of meaning. Knowing your purpose gives your life direction, determination, hope, and meaning.

Purpose that has a forceful impact on your life is three dimensional—incidental, individual, and universal. Incidental purpose is the motivation or reason for a specific action that you take. It is variable and changes from action to action or endeavor to endeavor. Incidental purpose dictates the goals and objectives that you set for a given project. It is the impetus for a particular pursuit that you may undertake, such as a college degree or an investment plan. It is specific to an incident in your life.

The second dimension of purpose is individual. Individual purpose is a life mission or calling. This does not mean that it has to be for a lifetime. Your calling may change as you mature, gain experience, and increase your knowledge. As you become better acquainted with your talents and abilities and develop spiritually, you will better understand your purpose. This clearer understanding could prompt you to change the direction of your life in response to the yearning of your soul.

The third dimension to purpose is universal. As the label suggests, universal purpose concerns your life's benefit to others and to your physical surroundings. It is frequently referred to as your "higher calling." That purpose is a universal one because it reaches beyond self in recognition that our lives are intertwined. There is no action that you as an individual can take that does not involve the life of another person. John Donne said it this way: "No man is an island, entire of itself. Every man is a piece of the continent, a part of the main." Universal purpose is your assignment of responsibility for the piece of the universe that you are. Everyone and everything that comes in touch with you should be enhanced, not diminished, by the connection.

Universal purpose is not predestination. It sets only the broad aim of beneficial interdependence. Your life pursuit to achieve that objective is a matter of choice. You choose your individual purpose. If what you choose to do is to be satisfying and provide you the sense that you are doing something meaningful, it must connect with universal purpose.

If you are to find pleasure in what you are doing, the incidental purpose must be congruent with your individual purpose. In other words, your day-to-day activities must be consistent with what you see and have chosen as your life mission. More significant, though, is that the power that comes from living in purpose will be ignited when your reason for doing what you do each day is not simply consistent but actually connected to your life mission.

Your quest is to know what your purpose is and to understand its significance to your environment. The question is whether you will set your course, make your choices, and act in connection with your purpose.

From the very moment that an apple seed begins to germinate, it grows and develops toward the purpose of producing apples. Even though the tree may not yield apples when it first takes on the form of a tree, it has the production of apples as its objective. Everything it does is apple-oriented. You can be like an apple seed and make everything you do purpose-oriented.

CHAPTER 18
CELEBRATING GIVING

Love, peace, happiness, kindness, and hope are gifts that you can give without losing what you possess for yourself. The more that you give to others, the more there is to share.

For several years, Jaci and I played the Santa Claus myth with our four children for Christmas until I tired of the long list of toys each child wanted. The lists seemed to grow longer every time. Not only did the cost of their wishes exceed my budget, but the children's behavior reflected the expectation of receiving rather than the anticipation of giving.

One year, Linnea, the youngest of the four, presented us with a list she developed from the Toys 'R' Us catalog complete with descriptions and prices. The total approached $500. I told her that Santa had a budget of $200 and she needed to make her list fit the budget. She did it without reluctance or pouting.

The following year, Jaci and I decided to tell the children that we were Santa and that we would give them the cash and let them buy whatever they wanted. This approach resulted in an unexpected benefit. I expected not to receive wish lists. I didn't expect that the children would immediately recognize the benefit of sharing and, eventually, the fun of giving.

In the first year of our new approach to experiencing Christmas giving with the children, Dana and Winter, the two oldest children, wanted the latest game console, controls, and cartridges. They did not have enough money to buy them individually. They decided to pool their money to buy the unit and a few game cartridges for them to share.

We have continued the practice of giving the children a Christmas allowance even though all four children are young adults and have their own jobs. We select names of family members for gift exchanges. Though we set a recommended amount to spend on the gift exchange, rarely do the children limit themselves to that amount even though the rest of the allowance can be spent on themselves. They don't even limit their giving to the family members whose names they select in the random drawing. Often they spend the entire allowance on gifts for family and friends. I am pleased with this Christmas spirit the family has learned—giving and sharing and being together as a family.

Why celebrate giving?

Giving, sharing, and serving are the actions that satisfy the yearning for significance. You were born to be significant. You were born to provide a contribution to the people with whom you come in contact and to your environment. The depth of your significance is best measured by what flows from you rather than what comes to you. Giving, sharing, and serving are the meaningful actions of the rest of the universal environment—the earth, the sky, the animals, the plants.

If you profess adherence to the teachings of Christ, you should not limit your celebration and spirit of giving to the Christmas season. In Luke's account of the life of Christ, he wrote (at Luke 6:38) that Jesus said, among other things, "Give and it shall be given unto you." It is an admonition that is not seasonal. If we cherish the opportunity to give only in December, what happens to the rest of the year? We get nothing because if no one is giving, then there is nothing to be received. Some may even resort to taking what is not theirs.

It does not matter whether or not your religion is based on the teachings of Christ or that you profess religion at all. Giving is a natural instinct. It is, therefore, reflected in all religious doctrine and in humanistic behavior. Because giving is a natural instinct, its meaningfulness is not limited to the exchange of tangible possessions. We can give encouragement. We can share ideas. Your ability to open your heart and soul to give to, share with, and serve another person enhances the meaningfulness of the relationships you establish.

A dedicated season for giving, such as Christmas, offers you a golden opportunity to test your relationship skills. Sending a greeting card to someone with whom contact has been absent for too long can open the door to a more direct and personal contact to renew a friendship, make an apology, and seek forgiveness. You can take the time to make a call or send a letter, an e-mail, or a text message to let someone know that even though you've been away or been busy, you are thinking of them. Because the nature of relationships exist as thoughts in your mind and stimuli of emotions, knowing that someone is thinking of you makes you feel good. You share that good feeling with others by letting them know that they are in your thoughts.

The ultimate gift is not monetary and cannot be sent in a message. It is to give of your life—that is, to take time to serve. You can volunteer for an organization that serves the homeless. You can do what eighty-nine-year-old Bob (see Chapter 4) does and visit convalescent or senior citizen homes to make conversation or to lead a group in singing. You can offer to substitute as an in-home care provider for a friend or family member; you will serve both the person cared for and the caregiver, the latter receiving a no-doubt much-deserved respite. Giving your time in service is the ultimate gift because in doing so, you sacrifice all other obligations and opportunities that would demand your time. It is the sacrifice that adds value to a gift.

When you give, you promote the growth and spreading of the object given. Politicians and business people would have you believe that if you give your money to the retail stores, you will promote the commercial economy. But if being a product purchaser is where your significance rests, your life will run out of meaning when you run out of money. What is it that you want to promote? If love, then give love. If peace, then give peace. If happiness, then make someone happy. If kind words, then speak kind words. If hope, then offer encouragement. Love, peace, happiness, kindness, and hope are gifts that you can give without losing what you possess for yourself. They are not scarce. The more that you give to others, the more there is to share.

CHAPTER 19
DISCOVERING YOUR PURPOSE

*Discovering purpose is not the end of the journey; it is the
ride that makes the journey enjoyable.*

On the bus to work a few years ago, I sat next to
Belinda. She was not a regular passenger on Commuter
Route 785, the last run of the morning to Los Angeles from
Lancaster. Had she been a regular, she would have known
that the first seat behind the driver was my usual spot, and I
usually sat there alone. I'm not sure why no one wanted to sit
next to me, but I only had a seatmate when every other seat
was occupied.

Belinda was already seated when I boarded the bus to
take my usual spot. We struck up conversation, and she told
me that normally she rode the sixth run, but that morning she
was running late.

Eventually I got to the question that I often pose to
various people, whether during in-depth conversation or
casual encounters at the store, bank, or post office.

"Do you like your job?" I asked. I was particularly
interested in Belinda's answer since her daily commute to and
from work took about five hours.

"I love my job," she retorted with ardor.

I was surprised by Belinda's answer. I was astonished by
the passion of her response.

My question to Belinda followed her explanation that
she was a clerk working for the Immigration and
Naturalization Service. She was responsible for sending out
letters of appointment to applicants for United States
citizenship.

I thought to myself, "How could she love such mundane,
low-level, thankless work?" I had to ask.

"Why do you love your job?"

"Because I get to help people realize their dreams. The people who apply have taken a step toward their dream of being a citizen of this country. I get to send out the letter that they have been waiting for—the letter giving them their citizenship appointment date."

Belinda explained to me that a big problem that she runs into is that often the applicant has changed his or her address between the time of application and the time their citizenship appointment date is set. It breaks her heart to have an appointment letter returned by the post office as undeliverable, so she takes great pains to ensure that she has the applicant's current address to receive the good news that she sends out.

I was impressed with the dedication Belinda had toward her work and the purpose she found in what she did as a federal civil servant.

How do you discover your purpose?

There is a reason for your being—being here, being now, being you. You are a vital part of the universe, and like all other parts of creation, you have a role to play. Consider what our world would be without the sun...without water...without trees...without birds...without rocks. These non-human parts of our world were created—pre-programmed, if you will—to give to and serve the universe. They fulfill their purpose without question and without fail.

You are no less important than a stone, an eagle, a bush, a drop of rain, or a ray of light. Your universal role—the one given to you when you were made a part of creation—is to give and to serve.

How you give and/or serve is unique to you. It is the individual purpose; the discovery of which is what makes living an exciting journey. You can and should approach each moment of your life with the enthusiasm and excitement that you get from visiting a place for the first time—the new things to see, the new people to meet, the new information to gain, the inspiration and creativity to spark. Look in every situation, old or new, for the opportunity to give and to serve.

Your individual purpose is unique, not because you have only one purpose, but because it is contained within your unique talents, abilities, and spirit. You can have multiple purposes in your lifetime. They can be manifested consecutively, but more often you will have several purposes evident at any given time. Consider the multiple purposes of rain, for example. It cleans the air, provides moisture to the earth, replenishes lakes.

You discover your individual purpose by doing. The more you do, the more experience you gain. The experience gives you information as to the talents and skills that you have and as to where you might be of service. Once you discover purposefulness in what you do, as did Belinda, you can do it over and over again and be satisfied. However, your willingness to try something new puts you in a position to learn more about yourself and how else you can be a benefit to your world.

Also by doing you can discover what is not purposeful for you. If you do it but you can't put your heart and soul into it, it is not your purpose. Fulfillment of purpose can come only when your soul is connected to what you do.

You discover your unique purpose by identifying your talents and abilities. Life would be frustrating and meaningless if you were placed in this world to provide a service but not given the tools by which to serve. Don't frustrate yourself needlessly by seeking to do something you were not designed to do. Identify your talents and abilities. Strengthen your skills. The talents, abilities, and skills that another person has are not for you. You shouldn't envy others for their talents. Your purpose may be different from theirs, so your talents must be different.

Talent is not just what we commonly recognize as artistic prowess, such as the ability to sing, act, dance, sculpt, and the like. It is any ability that you possess that you master with little effort. Your talent can be in planning or organizing or leading. You can be talented in cleaning, in cooking, or in caring for children. You may be a master at speaking, at investigating, or at analyzing. You may display prowess in counseling, encouraging, or comforting. You might be a talented teacher or a master mechanic. You might develop skills in any of these or still other areas through formal training or through experience.

When you have identified your talents, abilities, and skills, then you know what you have to give; all you need to do is to find someone to give it to. You define the areas in which you can be of service, and you serve. If you experience joy in your giving or serving, you have discovered purpose.

You discover your individual purpose by seeking to meet a need. If you find yourself in a position to observe a problem, search your soul to find whether you are the one to solve the problem. If the situation evokes your compassion and you have the wherewithal to give or the ability to serve, you have discovered purpose. Your purpose need not be the direct provider of the service; your purpose could be as the catalyst to solve the problem.

Sometimes it takes a tragedy to magnify a problem large enough for us to see it. Sometimes a situation has to be brought close to home before we can see a need. Nonetheless, if the adverse circumstances cause you to open your soul to give and/or to serve some cause, you have discovered purpose.

Perhaps the need has already been identified and has been brought to your attention by someone else. You can join an organization that gives to those in need or serves a cause for humanity or the environment. Such organizations can be religious or secular. Through your membership in the organization, you can discover and fulfill purpose.

You discover purpose through introspection and reflection. Purposefulness engages the mind and the soul as well as the body. To be purposeful, what you do must be mentally stimulating and emotionally satisfying. As you look into your own heart and soul, seek the answers to these questions:

❖ What have you done for someone else of which you are proud? In that moment, you were probably fulfilling purpose.

❖ What holds your interest? If what you do does not stimulate your interest but rather bores you, it is not likely to be purposeful for you.

❖ If you did not have to make money to meet your daily living needs, what work would you volunteer to do? The likelihood is great that you are fulfilling purpose when you do something because you want to do it and your only benefit from doing it is intangible.

The process of discovering purpose never ends. There is no time or stage of your life when or where you can say, "Ah, my search is over. I have found it." As long as you have something to give and as long as there is a need or cause to be served, there is purpose to be discovered. Discovering purpose is not the end of the journey; it is the ride that makes the journey enjoyable.

A bird does not sing because it has an answer. It sings because it has a song.

- Chinese Proverb

PART V:
DEFINING YOURSELF

A gem is not polished without rubbing, nor a man perfected without trials.

- Chinese Proverb

CHAPTER 20
MEANINGFULNESS: SELF-DEFINITION

*Together your beliefs, desires, and principles of conduct
point your life in one direction or another. They define who
you are.*

In 1997, I was invited by the counseling staff of
Antelope Valley High School in Lancaster, California, to
present a workshop for ninth-grade students on motivation
and self-esteem. As an exercise for completion and
discussion in the forum, I gave the students a list of twenty
beliefs with which they could agree or disagree. I asked them
to strike out the statements with which they disagreed. I
asked them then to rank the importance of the beliefs that
remained and to identify the belief with which they most
strongly agreed. The list included:

1. All the power that I need is within me.
2. What I feel is not important; it is what I think that
   will get me success.
6. Who I know is more important than what I know.
7. God is.
9. The possibilities are unlimited.
11. Only I can determine my success and happiness.
14. Life is unfair.
16. My potential to succeed is determined by my
    race.
17. I am an important part of this world.
20. If I have enough money, I will be happy.

I was surprised to find that a large majority of students
retained Statement 14, "Life is unfair." I was shocked to find

that a solid majority of those who retained Statement 14 chose it as the one with which they most strongly agreed.

In an effort to learn more about what the teenagers believed and what experiences they had which led to the belief that life is unfair, I started a discussion about unfairness. To reach an understanding, I asked two questions, What is fair? and What would make life fair to you? There were few answers. The students expressed a general feeling that life is unfair. I became concerned that the decisions these youngsters would make and the actions they would take would be guided by their belief in the unfairness of life. I wondered how much of the good things in life they would miss because they didn't expect them to happen.

What beliefs and principles define who you are and what you will do?

Every decision you make and every action you take are influenced by what you hold in your mind and heart. Your beliefs, desires, and principles of conduct determine the direction in which you move at every decision point. If your life is to be meaningful, the set of beliefs you adopt, the desires you pursue, and the principles you adhere to must point you in the direction of meaningfulness.

The definition of who you are and the direction in which your life moves are ruled by your beliefs. Your beliefs provide the attitudinal framework for your desires and behavior. If you believe that life is unfair, you will expect to encounter unfairness in the situations in which you find yourself and acquiesce in its occurrence. You are likely not to pursue fairness. You may even perpetrate acts of unfairness believing that unfairness is the rule of the game.

In contrast, if you believe that there is a purpose for your life, you will act purposefully. You will seek to discover and fulfill your purpose. When you are presented with choices, you will choose that which allows you to fulfill your purpose.

Even faced with what appears to be adversity, you are able to look at a situation to find how it can contribute to purposeful living.

While beliefs define your attitude, desire sets the course that you will take. If you want to be a doctor, you don't apply to law school. If you are single and want to be married, you seek out and woo spousal prospects. You have to know what you want to know where to go to get it.

Desires aren't pursued in a vacuum, however. They are governed by your beliefs. That is to say, your desire must have a context, and that context dictates the course of your life. Your desire to win in the context of a belief that everyone can win will send you in a different direction than it would in the context of a belief that life is unfair. Believing that everyone can win, your desire to win might lead you to share your winning knowledge with everyone with whom you come in contact. On the other hand, if you believe that life is unfair, you may be compelled to conceal what you know about winning to give yourself the winning advantage.

The actions you will take in the pursuit of your desires are delineated by the principles you adopt. Principles of conduct establish the boundaries over which you will not cross no matter the course your beliefs and desires dictate. If you adopt excellence as a principle to govern your performance, you will give your best effort and seek to improve. You will not accept mediocrity. If integrity is one of your principles, no one will be able to pay you to compromise your moral values.

You acquire your rules of conduct from various sources. They may come from your upbringing at home. They may come from religious teachings. Through your formal education or through your interactions with other people, you develop moral standards and a sense of right and wrong. When you enter a profession, you may adopt the established professional ethics. Your job may set work ethics for you. When you adopt rules of conduct as principles to guide your life, they become the basis for making decisions when you are presented with choices of what to do. When you compromise those principles, you are in effect creating for yourself new rules of conduct.

Little of what I have discussed here regarding beliefs, desires, and principles of conduct will be relevant to you if you view life as a conglomeration of events that happen to you. All you do is wait to see what happens and move in the direction in which you are pushed. The direction your life takes is determined by circumstances. However, if you believe that life is a collection of activities that you choose, your beliefs, desires, and principles of conduct will determine the meaningfulness of life.

Together your beliefs, desires, and principles of conduct define who you are. We can recognize and know the person called Don Williams, for example, based on the characteristics that we attribute to him, just as we recognize the animal called "tiger" from the characteristics we learn that are associated with that animal. Your outward appearance, your conversation, your thoughts and emotions, and your behavior tell us who you are. If you change what you believe or the desires you pursue or the principles that guide you, you change how you are defined.

CHAPTER 21
SETTING YOUR PERSPECTIVE

Your perspective on life is the basis for defining who you are.

Retirement has become a frequent conversation among my colleagues at work. Each of us has reached or is fast approaching fifty-five, the determinative age. Some set the date of their retirement after calculating their monthly retirement benefit. Others set the date based on when the kids will finish college or when the mortgage will be paid off.

I asked one colleague who had announced his retirement about the number of years he had worked on the job. He responded, "Twenty-six years. Twenty-six wasted years of my life."

I was sad for him as I considered the amount of time he had given to his employment. As I pondered his response, I began to consider more than the time. Were there no events on the job that gave him joy? Did he not hear a case and write a decision that had a positive impact on the lives of a family? Were his relationships with his colleagues, including me, meaningless? It wasn't just time on a job. Twenty-six years of his life involved activities, events, and people. Was it all wasted?

How do you see your life?

After reading this sentence, pause a moment and recall as much as you can of the last thirty days of your life—what you did, why you did it, where you were, people involved, how you felt, what you learned. Now consider the different ways in which you can characterize life. While you did what you did, you gained knowledge and expressed emotions, suggesting that life is a body-mind-soul interaction. Things happened to and around you, justifying the view that life is a chain of events. While events occurred, you were engaged in various activities; life, then, can be seen as a collection of activities. As you were doing things, you were interacting with other people, establishing the notion that life is a network of relationships. Engaging in these events, activities, and relationships, you continually made choices, offering evidence that life is a system of options and decisions. One month passed with thoughts and emotions, events, activities, relationships, and decisions, so life can be considered as time.

In his poem "The Blind Men and the Elephant," John Godfrey Saxe illustrated how definitions can vary depending on one's perspective. The first blind man felt the broad side of the elephant and said it was like a wall. The second felt the smooth, sharp tusk and described it as a spear. The next man handled the squirming trunk and concluded that the elephant was like a snake. The next blind man touched the animal about the knee and thought the beast to be like a tree. The fifth grabbed the ear and said the elephant resembled a fan. The sixth man groped the swinging tail and thought the elephant to be like a rope.

We are much like the six blind men when we attempt to describe life. We never get to see the whole thing; that is, our view is always a retrospective one, being certain only of what has already occurred. Hence, we develop our opinion based on the focus of our past.

You can explain life as passive in terms of what is happening to you or as active in terms of what you are doing. How you view the nature of life will determine the value you place on it and, as a consequence, your attitude toward others and how you interact with them. Your perspective on life is the basis for defining who you are. Your personal view of life is the context of your beliefs and principles by which you act. Because your focus on life changes, the way you define or describe life can change.

You might view your life as the union of forces of the universe. It is the manifestation of forces of nature coming together as one being. You are that unique being created by the physical force experienced in body, the intelligent force experienced in mind, and the spiritual force experienced in soul.

You had nothing to do with the forces of the universe coming together to be you. You could not have had a role because you did not exist until the union occurred. You can, however, control the impact and interaction of these forces in your life. You operate the dials that determine your emphasis on body, mind, and soul. You control the balance of the physical, mental, and emotional aspects of your life. Because it is tangible and, therefore, more readily understood, the physical aspect of life may get more of your attention. However, when you define yourself in terms of life's three dimensions of body, mind, and soul, you recognize the value of having the appropriate balance among your physical, mental, and spiritual being.

You might view life as time. Time is that segment of eternity during which your soul, mind, and body join to interact with the universe. Viewing life as time enables you to quantify it, measure its passing, and treat it as a commodity to be traded on the open market. Is the value of your life $10 per hour, $100 per hour, $1,000 per hour, or more?

When you treat life as a temporal commodity, you may be inclined to treat it as though the supply is plentiful. So long as you are conscious that the hands on the clock face are still moving or that the digits on the clock display are changing, you believe that you have time. You may live with the cavalier attitude, There is more where that came from. When you define yourself in terms of time, your desires, beliefs, and principles will not reflect the urgency of making each moment meaningful until you feel that your time is running out.

You might view life as a system of options and decisions. At each instant of your existence you have an option. At the basic level, the option is to continue what you are doing or to do something else. If you choose to continue doing what you do, you also make the decision to forego all other options. When you choose to do something else, the decision-making becomes more complex because of the many options available to you. To make the right choices, you must develop your decision-making skills.

At the basic level of option and decision, you are in complete control. One option you always have is to relinquish your control to someone else or to the circumstances. Even if you choose to relinquish control, you always have the option to retake control and be the captain of your own fate. In other words, you no longer allow circumstances to dictate to you or to let another person decide for you. A meaningful life in the context of options and decisions requires that you focus on your desires and beliefs at each decision point.

You might view life as a chain of events. An event is the set of circumstances in which you find yourself. The set includes the orientation points used by psychiatrists of time, place, person, and things. Each set of circumstances involves a segment of your life; it does not matter the length. Such segment represents the time element of the set of circumstances. The physical location where the event occurs provides the place circumstance. There will be a component that can be expressed in terms of other people. That expression can be that you are alone—that is, there are no other people. Finally, objects, including living things other than people, are the things of the circumstance.

Your events of today are linked to those of yesterday. Even though you may have begun today with the idea of a fresh start, today's circumstances have a historical connection to yesterday. The events of your life are linked whether you look at them day by day, year by year, or second by second.

Events are linked together by one or more of the circumstantial elements of time, place, person, or things. So long as you are involved in the picture, so to speak, all the events of your life are linked. Your current event has a connection to a past event and a future one. There must always be a transitional connection from one event to another. You are the person that provides the circumstantial link to a series of events. The time, place, other people, and things may change. The time can change while the people, place, and things remain the same from one event to another. Since time is constantly changing, no two events of your life can involve the identical set of circumstances.

Events can occur over which you exercise no control of the time, place, people, and things. That is to say, you may find yourself in a set of circumstances that you cannot alter. You can, however, retain control by extricating yourself from the situation. (My discussion about control here assumes that you are physically and mentally capable of exercising your will and are not held against your will by another person.)

On the other hand, there are times when you control the setting. You choose the time, the place, the people, and the things that will be the circumstances of your event. When you look at life as a chain of events, you can define yourself in terms of the principles that make each event significant to living meaningfully.

You might view life as a network of relationships. Every instant of your existence can be described in terms of relationships with other people. Your relationship with mother was created the instant of your conception. Throughout your life you form relationships, and you continue to establish them until you die. (See Chapter 13 for a discussion of various types of relationships.)

Some of your relationships are formed without your initiative. Examples are parents, siblings, and other biological connections. Other examples are your gender connection as female or male and your association with a particular ethnic group.

Other relationships may or may not be of your choosing. Your neighbors or your coworkers are examples of such relationships. If you live in a particular location and someone moves into the house next door to you, you have neighbors that are not of your own choosing. If, on the other hand, you do the moving, you can choose who your neighbors will be. Similarly, you have no active role in forming relationships with coworkers if you are working on a job where someone else does the hiring and you have no input. If you are doing the hiring or if you are seeking a job, you will have some say in who will be your colleague.

Finally, there are relationships that are formed only through your initiative. A friendship cannot be established without your willingness to do so. You choose the people with whom you want to socialize.

I have yet to hear any expression of meaningfulness that did not involve one's relationships to other people. A perspective on life as a network of relationships sets the context for your principles for personal interactions.

You might view life as a collection of activities. It is the sum of what you do between birth and death. Your being is heightened by your doing. You make life meaningful by choosing to do meaningful things.

None of the six perspectives on life discussed above preclude another. Each perspective has applicability in understanding life, in defining who we are, and in making life meaningful.

Your body, with the instinct for survival, will seek to extend life in this physical realm as long as possible. Your mind, on the other hand, understands that your time here on earth is limited. It knows mortality. Because you understand that just to be born and then to die is meaningless, your mind reflects on what happens in between to find some value. Meanwhile, there is a spiritual force operating within your soul that concerns itself with connection—connection to others, connection to the universe, and connection with the power of eternity. Making life meaningful is to strike the right balance of physical, mental, and spiritual interaction in the brief time that you are on earth. When you successfully strike such balance, you can make the decisions in every event of your life to do the things that connect you with your spot in the universe.

If there is bitterness in the heart, sugar in the mouth won't make life sweeter.

- Jewish Proverb

CHAPTER 22
DEFINING MOMENTS

You are defined by what you believe, the emotions you express, and the principles that guide your actions and your interactions with others.

I earned my spending money when I was a child by doing chores in the house or in the yard for neighbors. I got a quarter here and a quarter there for moving furniture, for taking trash out and putting trash cans away, for raking up leaves and fallen fruit from backyard trees, and for sweeping sidewalks and driveways. The Colemans, Brutons, Boyds, and Abatias often found small jobs for me to do.

Maude Riley also gave me tasks to do around her house. She often gave me jobs that other neighbors didn't seem willing to let a blind boy try. She handed me pruning shears and showed me how to clip the rosebushes. She taught me the difference by feel between the good plants and the weeds as we cleaned out her flowerbeds. Once I went to her house and found her painting her living room. She invited me in and immediately put me to work. She put a roller in my hand, showed me where the pan of paint and the stepladder were, and asked me to paint the ceiling.

I don't remember getting money from Maude. She fed me, and while we worked together, I got conversation, instruction, and advice. "Don't let one monkey stop the show," Maude would say when I talked about a girl I liked who didn't seem to like me. We talked about our relationships with God and our churches, and she voiced her opinions about the racial tension in the country. The nature and topic of the conversation changed from visit to visit, but one piece of advice was constant and frequent. Whenever Maude gave me a job to do, inside the house or outside, she would say:

If a job is once begun,
Leave it not until it's done;
Be the task great or small,
Do it well or not at all.

Maude's constant repetition of this poem left an imprint in my mind—an impression that is the basis of my commitment to excellence.

Who are you?

You are defined by what you believe, the emotions you express, and the principles that guide your actions and your interactions with others. You reveal your beliefs, emotions, and principles to yourself and to others by what you do. When they are first revealed to you through some situation or event, it is a defining moment.

A defining moment is an experience or event that is the source of a principle or belief that now guides your thinking and actions. Every moment of your life is an opportunity for you to define who you are. From each of your experiences you can either discover more about yourself—your thinking, your feelings, your attitudes—or further develop and clarify what you already know. You should not let a moment go by that you do not add definition to your uniqueness and individualism.

A defining moment need not be an "aha" moment. An "aha" response usually comes from a purposeful search to understand something about yourself. When you make your discovery and come to the understanding that you seek, you have reached "aha." Sometimes, however, you begin with the understanding and through reflection want to trace the origin of a particular personality trait. The original moment may be defining, but because the definition occurred over time, it does not cause you to say, "Aha!"

Sometimes a light flashes on immediately and unexpectedly and reveals something divinely important about who you are. When it does, your mind is opened to something about your life that forever changes the course that it takes. You have then had an epiphany. An epiphany is always a defining moment.

Misfortune is often a place where we will learn new things about what we believe and feel and establish rules that will guide all future behavior. An experience of tragedy might be the only way to get your attention and to make you stop and think about what you are doing with your life. If you emerge from the experience with a better understanding of who you are and your purpose in life, calling the experience a misfortune or a tragedy is a misnomer. The experience is a defining moment. All experiences that add definition to you are valuable experiences, and you are fortunate to have gone through them.

A defining moment is life-changing, but all life-changing moments are not defining. An essential characteristic of life is change. When change ceases, death occurs. Hence, every experience in life is an experience of change. But the change may not define you. It could just be the result of what you already know about your beliefs, thoughts, feelings, and attitudes. For example, taking a promotion at your job that necessitates moving from Arizona to Wyoming will change your life, but may not add definition to who you are. Decisions that you make that result in significant alterations in the course of your life—taking a promotion, moving to another state, starting a business, getting married, adopting a child, going to college, retiring, and so on—are directional moments. They become defining moments when as a result of them you adopt or alter what you believe or you establish new principles that guide your future decisions and actions. In other words, a moment that alters the course of your life is a directional moment; a moment that alters your principles or beliefs is a defining moment.

A memorable moment is not necessarily a defining moment. You may never forget the time you went to the casino and hit a jackpot of ten thousand dollars, but how did it define you? An experience may leave a lasting impression in your mind for many reasons. It could be because of the emotion it evoked; it could be the permanent physical impact it had; it could be the knowledge you gained; it could be the relationship you established as a result of the encounter. If the lasting memory does not carry with it a lesson learned that impacts what you believe and the principles by which you live, it is a memorable moment but not a defining moment.

Any experience that you have that results in your discovering a purpose in your life is a defining moment. Purpose has a fundamental impact on your beliefs, feelings, and attitudes.

Often people ask themselves, What is life? This philosophical query has been posed by thinkers well known and perhaps the unknown thinkers such as yourself. Your defining moments do not necessarily offer an answer to the question, What is life? They do answer the question, What is my life? or Who am I?

There is no single moment in your life that defines you, so you need not search for The Defining Moment. You are a continually evolving individual, and moment by moment your identity is defined. One defining moment is no more or less important than another. All of them are essential stages of the development of your uniqueness.

CHAPTER 23
BELIEVING IS SEEING

You can set your view of life based on what has happened to you, or you can use your hopes and dreams as the backdrop for your vision.

In 1967, Althea, a woman I met at a leadership conference, told me about her father's becoming blind. She recounted how active her father had been for most of his life—into his sixties. Then he lost his sight. When he did, his life took a one hundred eighty-degree turn. He sat at home and did nothing. His wife and children could not coax him into participating in any kind of activity. After his blindness, Althea's father's life was over, or so it appeared that he considered it to be.

Clarissa had a different story to tell me five years later when we were at Yale together. Her father had been without use of his eyes several years before she knew that he was blind. She said that the only difference in her father's activities that she witnessed was that he did not get up in the morning and go out to a job. Around the house he continued to work with his tools repairing damage to the house and furniture; he worked in the yard. Clarissa recounted one time when her father was doing some electrical repair work. Working to reconnect wires, he asked her to tell him the colors.

"What color is this one?" he asked her.

"It's white."

"And what about this one?" he asked again.

"That's red," the three-year-old child responded.

Clarissa explained that she thought her dad was asking the questions just to test her knowledge of colors. She had no idea that he was asking because he could no longer see.

Unlike Althea's father and Clarissa's father, I lost my sight when I was just a young child. I was running backwards on the sidewalk across the street from my house. I fell on the back of my head. The injury was severe, blood spilling out both on the sidewalk and on me. I was taken to the local hospital where the doctors stitched up my head wound and sent me home. The severity of the accident and injury came to light later. The impact of my head with the concrete walkway caused my retinas to detach. I was blind. Subsequent surgery restored sight to my right eye, but I gradually lost sight in that eye again.

I adjusted well to being blind. In fact, I can't remember much about being able to see with both eyes, having used them for only four years. For me, being without the use of my eyes seems quite natural.

Given my quick adjustment to blindness, for a long time I believed that a person's ability to adjust to losing sight depended on how long he or she lived with the use of eyes. As I considered the stories of Althea and Clarissa and the lives of other blind people with whom I went to school, I have formed a different opinion. What a person who is blind does with his or her life is not different from what a sighted individual does with his or hers. Whether blind or sighted, life becomes what an individual believes life should be.

What do you believe your life to be?

Life is what you believe it to be. Your belief becomes the lens through which you see the circumstances around you, what happens to you, the opportunities you find in the circumstances, and the lessons you learn from your experiences.

If you ascribe to the notion that life is difficult, you are likely to acquiesce in the unfortunate outcome of a tough situation. If you believe that life is complex, you will look for the complication in what is meant to be simple. If you think that life sucks, you'll expect the worst to happen.

You are responsible for establishing your view of life. You can look at your unfortunate experiences and create a negative view of life, or you can focus on the good things that have happened and treat the unfortunate events as exceptions. You can set your view of life based on what has happened to you, or you can use your hopes and dreams as the backdrop for your vision. If you abdicate your responsibility to consciously choose, you will end up accepting someone else's vision for your life.

You can treat your life like a rosebush. When you look at a rosebush in the springtime, you see buds and flowers. They can be of various colors—purple, red, pink, white, yellow, or orange. Emotionally, if not verbally, you react to what you see with "that is beautiful." The beauty of what you see is not diminished by the fact that the same bush that bears the flowers has thorns that can cause sharp pain. Having seen one, touched one, smelled one, received one, or given one, you have come to know the beauty in a rose. Notwithstanding the presence of thorns and the possibility of aphids and weeds, there is no meaning in the declaration, A rose is difficult.

To adjudge that something is difficult, you must be familiar with ease. To determine that something is complex, you must have a concept of simplicity. If you can tell when your life sucks, then you should be able to tell when it's awesome, cool, or the bomb. Take your familiarity and knowledge of what is easy, simple, and/or cool to reset your view of life.

Life is like the rose. The nature of it is not defined by the pain and struggle involved in cultivating it. Life is intrinsically valuable. That value is what gives life its significance. Create for yourself a view of life that always allows you to assess the value in each of your experiences. This ability will allow you to make your life meaningful.

If you believe in the meaningfulness of your life, you will strive to make each moment meaningful. Every breath you take should be full of meaning. Every time your heart beats, it will beat with meaning. You will think and feel with meaning in mind and soul. You won't look for meaning. You will make it.

PART VI:
WHAT GETS IN THE WAY

The grass is always greener on the other side of the fence.
                                    - American Proverb

CHAPTER 24
BEING DISTRACTED

*Without purpose to guide your choices, you will be easily
allured by what is pleasing for the moment.*

Several years ago, I worked with James, whose job was
to represent his employer in the administrative hearings over
which I presided. His position being one that did not require a
background in law, I was curious as to how he came to
perform that job. One day we had some time outside a
hearing, so I asked the question to satisfy my curiosity, "How
did you come to be an appeals representative?"

James explained that after graduating from college with
a bachelor's degree, he was tired of having no money. He
applied for an entry-level position in social services just to
make some money, fully intending to go back to school to get
his master's degree in English. Once he had the job and
money that he didn't have before, he rented an apartment and
bought a car. Eventually he obtained a credit card for the
convenience of buying gas for the car. He found himself with
monthly food, clothing, shelter and transportation bills, which
required that he continue working to pay them. Then job
promotions with the opportunity to make more money
became available, and he applied for them. He eventually
promoted to be an appeals representative. It wasn't the job he
really wanted. He wanted to be an English teacher. James
told me that he was going to go back to school once his bills
were paid.

I asked James, "When will your bills be paid? When will
you not need shelter, food, clothes, and transportation?"

I didn't see James for several months after our
conversation. I asked a colleague of his where he was. The

colleague told me that James quit the job to go to graduate school.

What is distracting you from fulfilling your dream? More important, what is distracting you from living your purpose?

It may be that you are not living your purpose and experiencing meaningfulness in your life because of distractions. You can be distracted by money. You can be distracted by image. You can be distracted by possessions. You can be distracted by entertainment. You can be distracted by relationships. You can be distracted by obligations. Any or all of these can become your focus of living and consume your time, so that there is no life left for serving your purpose.

Money may be the most alluring distraction. With it you can magnify your image, obtain possessions, and pay for whatever entertainment you desire. Your money might even get you into the relationship that you think will make you happy. Today our society, no matter how provincial or global the prospective, functions by money. You need money for shelter, food, clothing, health care, and transportation—the basics for survival. You must give time to making money in order to maintain life. However, money becomes a distraction to your living meaningfully when it becomes the end for what you do rather than a means for obtaining the basic necessities. As your pile of money grows, your definition of what is needed expands. As your needs expand, your need to make more money also grows. This continuous process can pull you further and further away from living with purpose.

To avoid being distracted by money, you must learn to pare down your needs. The two tools to use to trim down your needs and, as a result, your need to make more money are these questions: Do I need it in order to survive? Do I need it in order to fulfill my purpose? If you don't get a "yes" to one of these questions, then the item is a want. Your choice then boils down to whether you want money or you want meaning.

Even if money is not your focus, your image can distract you from your life's purpose. Image can be a matter of appearance or a matter of reputation or a matter of status. Whatever time you spend on how you look or the level of your status in the community is time taken away from acting to fulfill your purpose. You can miss your full joy of life by choosing your life encounters based on what other people think of you or think you should be doing. To prevent this distraction, your ear should be attuned more to the voice of purpose than the voices of other people.

If you own stuff you don't use, if you buy just to have the latest, or if you have more possessions than you have place to store them, you have laid up for yourself great potential for distraction. Time to keep it clean, keep it up, and keep it safe is time lost from serving your purpose. Worry about someone taking your property displaces space in your heart for reflection and/or creativity. The same tools you use to pare down your needs, you can use to strip away unnecessary stuff. If you are holding on to stuff that is not needed for your survival and not needed to fulfill your purpose, you are holding the potential for distraction.

When you watch TV or rush to the latest movie opening, are you furthering the goals that bring meaning to your life? It is okay for the answer to this question to be no. It is okay that you seek entertainment for entertainment's sake. However, for the growth and development that will make life meaningful, you must moderate the time you spend being entertained just as you would moderate your intake of sweets. Like eating a delicious meal, watching television may be pleasing, but spending too much time doing so may not be healthy. You may be distracted from the life you were meant to live.

It might be people, rather than things, that distract you from living with meaning. The relationships that you should retain are those from which the two of you derive a benefit— that is, in which you both find support toward your goals of living meaningfully. The time you spend nurturing and developing such beneficial relationships is time well spent. It is a distraction from purposeful living when you spend time with people who are using you and/or who are draining you emotionally and from whom you gain no benefit.

You can also be distracted by your own sense of obligation to do something for someone that is not congruent with your purpose. Perhaps you committed to taking on a job that you now find is not allowing you to live purposefully. If this is your situation, you must assess whether the loss in your reputation you will experience from breaking the commitment is greater than the gain you will experience from moving in the direction of your heart's desire. If the loss of reputation is great, you may wish to serve out your commitment. Perhaps someone has placed on you a sense of obligation through a guilt trip, so you accept the responsibility to assuage your guilt. You should never feel guilty about saying no to taking on responsibilities that distract you from fulfilling your purpose.

You are subject to distractions if you don't know your purpose. Without purpose to guide your choices of your life's activities, you can be easily allured by what is pleasing for the moment. You can be misled by what others believe would be best for you.

To avoid being distracted from what is meaningful for your life, you must know your purpose, know your desires, set your priorities, and adjust your balance. None of these are once-in-a-lifetime activities. Purpose and desires can change, so priorities and balance must be reset. You must decide how often you will need to reflect and re-evaluate for change and adjustments.

CHAPTER 25
MAKING A LIVING

When you can make both meaning and money from your
work, then you are really living.

I sat down in the first seat behind the driver, getting comfortable for my two-hour ride to work when I found myself as an eavesdropper on a conversation between two women. I don't know their names, so I'll call them Jean and Gayle.

Gayle, sitting across the aisle from me said, "Mine is a light grayish green. Sometimes when you look at it, it looks gray, but when the sun shines directly on it, it's green."

"Mine is too," Jean, sitting directly behind me, responded excitedly.

For a split second I considered injecting my comments into the conversation because my Ford Windstar minivan, based on my wife's description, was the same color that Gayle had described. I felt like conversation that morning and would have gladly shared my experiences with the Ford Windstar, which I had purchased in December 2000.

Jean then spoke again and immediately made my contribution to the conversation insignificant. "It's the second Jag that I bought. I just had to have me another one."

I was grateful for my hesitation to get into another's conversation uninvited. It saved me a great deal of embarrassment. In terms of social status, my Windstar could not compare to a Jaguar.

I immediately saw what I believed to be a sad irony in that these two women were starting what would probably be a thirteen-hour commute-and-work day on a bus so that they could afford to park expensive cars in their garages. As I began to set up my Sudoku board to work a puzzle on my way to work, I mused about when Jean and Gayle would drive their Jags. Not to work obviously. To church maybe? To the grocery store? Just to some special event? Was it worth getting up at five o'clock each day to go to work?

Why are you working at your job?

Making a living is likely the greatest barrier to your living meaningfully. If the only reason that you are going to work for someone else day after day or spending long hours in your own business is to have an income, you are methodically building a wall that separates the life that you are living from the one you are supposed to live. Making a living can get in the way of your living with purpose in several ways.

Making a living can distract you from living purposefully when getting money becomes the reason for your being. In a money-based economy, you must make money to purchase your necessities of life—food, clothing, shelter, health care, transportation. Once you are assured enough money to provide the basics for today, you look to the future. A little more money and you won't have to worry about what you'll eat, what you'll wear, and where you'll sleep tomorrow. With just a bit more money, you can supersize it. Eat more; eat out; eat steak instead of beans. No more secondhand or hand-me-downs for you; you must buy the best clothes. Why rent a one-bedroom apartment when you can own the three-bedroom house? Sarah Jones has a new car; why shouldn't you get one too? It doesn't matter that you don't have the money to buy one. You can get a loan. You can keep working to pay it off. As your debt for today's wants mount, you look for a different job that pays more. And the cycle continues.

Wait a minute. There are future needs, or are they wants? What are they now? You have to save money for the kids' college...for your retirement. Gosh! You'll have to make more money so that what you stash away for retirement will support you at the level to which you have become accustomed. Take the job. So what if you hate it. The money's good and it has good benefits—health and pension. If you could just pick the right six numbers, you wouldn't have to work at all. It's all about the money.

Making a living can distract you from your purpose to give and to serve. To be successful at making a living, as the general population views success, you must put yourself into a get-and-accumulate mode. You'll get up early in the morning, you'll take a two-hour commute on the train, and/or you'll fight the traffic into town because your reward will be to get more for you and your family. To put forth this effort for the purpose of giving to and/or serving another person might be the last thing you'd consider. In fact, you might even feel in competition with everyone else who is also struggling to survive, so giving or helping them would work against your self-interest.

Making a living can cause you to waste life on meaningless pursuits. If you have a job at which you spend eight hours a day, five days a week, you have devoted to that job a third of your life. (The latter assertion takes into account the time it takes to prepare for work and the commute time.) Another one third of your life may be devoted to sleeping. You have just a third of your life remaining to devote to all other activities and endeavors, including family interaction, social gathering, church, community, spiritual and personal development, and financial and legal matters. In which third of your life do you have time to discover and fulfill your purpose? When it comes to dedicating life to various activities, it is a zero-sum game. Giving more time to one activity requires taking away time from another. If the work you have chosen as a way to make a living is not meaningful, you have devoted a significant part of your life to meaninglessness.

Making a living can undermine your priorities. Living with purpose requires that purpose be the leading consideration in all that you choose to do. If money, not purpose, is the reason you took the job you have, your priorities have been hijacked. It is no wonder that you reach a crisis point in your life when you wake up to the fact that life has no meaning for you. Meaning was not a priority and it continued to lose rank as other things captured your attention.

Making a living can stifle creativity. The rote of getting up, going to work, coming home, sleeping, and getting up again to go to work will disengage your mind and imagination. You develop a habit of going to work. Your car may seem to be on automatic driver and gets you to your work site without your thinking about where you are going and how you are getting there. If your mind and imagination are not engaged, there can be no creativity. Similarly, creativity may be lacking because you haven't time for it. You have filled your day up with too much stuff to take the time to think, engage, reflect, and imagine.

Making a living can suppress your talents and abilities. If your job is to be meaningful to you, it must allow you to use and hone your talents and skills. If you are working and you don't know what your talents are, you are a living testament to the notion that making a living suppresses your talents. The pursuit to which you devote as much as a third of your adult life should afford you the opportunity to discover your uniqueness and value. When will you do it if you don't do it now?

Making a living can cause you to develop fear of uncertainty. A derivative goal of making a living is job security. You seek to be secure in your position as the assurance that you will have the wherewithal to meet your needs and pay your debts. The longer you stay in such a position of security, the less likely you are to take risks and try something new.

Making a living lures you into complacency. It's what you are expected to do. It's expected by your family and by society. So you do it. Even if you don't like what you do, you are not moved to do something about it—that is, to make the change that will make you happy. You continue to do what you do because that's the way it is.

Making a living can cause you to live outside your purpose. If you are not working to give and serve as your creator endowed you to do, you have devoted your life to living outside your purpose. You might gain a benefit from what you do, but you lose the greater benefit of what you were supposed to do. The universe loses as a result.

Making a living can limit your opportunities. What would you do if you didn't have to make money? Your answers to this question will provide you a list of the opportunities that you forego because you are making a living.

Making a living may disengage the soul from living. If you cannot put your heart and soul into your job, you have disengaged your soul so that you can report to work everyday. You'll never feel the joy that life is supposed to be or experience self-fulfillment if your soul is not engaged in what you do.

Making a living can dull your sensitivity to the needs of others. If you are operating on the get-and-accumulate mode and your soul is not engaged, you will not be able to feel the empathy that prompts you to respond to the needs of another person. You begin to believe that it's not your responsibility to care; every man must take individual responsibility and get his own.

You can circumvent the barrier between making a living and living with purpose by setting meaningfulness instead of money as your priority when choosing a job. When you can make both meaning and money from your work, then you are really living.

CHAPTER 26
LIVING THROUGH AVOIDANCE

Living through avoidance will keep you wondering what might have been if you had only taken a chance.

I discovered that I wasn't the only guy who had a romantic interest in Clarissa when I visited her in her dormitory room one evening. There was quite a crowd already assembled—Frank, Earl, and Phil. I went to Clarissa's dorm under the pretext of wanting to watch the news on television.

In those college days at Yale in the early seventies, few students had their own television. If you wanted to watch TV, you'd go to the TV room set up in each residential college. Clarissa was one of the exceptions; she had her own television.

I didn't really care about the TV or the news. I wanted to be in the same room with Clarissa. I learned that Earl and Frank and Phil also wanted to be in her company.

I had no expectation that Clarissa, a kind and intelligent graduate student, would choose me over the other options apparently available to her. My belief was that I, with my blindness, could not win over three sighted men, all of whom were also students at Yale.

To avoid what I expected to be the inevitable rejection, I stopped visiting Clarissa. I avoided going to the dining hall at the times when we usually met for dinner. I went to Macy's and bought a TV to put in my room, and there I watched TV alone. Loneliness was what I got in my effort to avoid rejection.

What are you avoiding?

All the things that you do in this life are the result of your seeking pleasure and/or avoiding pain. Your decision to take or not take a given action or to engage or not in a particular activity is based on a pleasure-pain analysis. If you determine that the activity would be pure pleasure, you are very likely to do it. If, on the other hand, you determine that the activity would be painful, you will not get involved. You are presented with a challenge when the activity could bring both pain and pleasure. You then have to decide whether you are willing to pay the price of pain for the pleasure that you may derive from your action.

As a physical survival mechanism, we have been equipped with an automatic reflex to avoid pain. The instant we experience pain or discomfort, we seek to stop or relieve it. Unless you were born with an impaired reflex mechanism, the very first time you touched a hot stove, you immediately withdrew from the source of pain. Because you can remember the discomfort, you have avoided touching hot objects ever since. In the same way that you learned about the pain of being burned, you have learned the other physical limitations you have. That is, you've learned what things cause pain, and you avoid them.

Avoiding emotional pain is as natural as avoiding physical pain. The problem in our effort to avoid emotional pain is that there cannot be 100-percent certainty that pain will occur in a given situation. You can be sure that if you touch hot metal, it will burn and you will feel pain. However, you cannot be sure that the pain of rejection will not occur if you, for example, engage in a hot relationship. One way to be 100-percent certain to avoid the pain of rejection is to avoid placing yourself in the position of being rejected. When you take this approach to avoid pain, you are living through avoidance.

Two major sources of emotional pain are guilt and rejection. The possibility of feeling guilt or the possibility of being rejected will cause us to limit our actions and to avoid situations that may result in either of these painful experiences.

Guilt is the pain that comes from doing something wrong. The extent to which you will feel guilt depends on your sense of what's right and what's wrong. If your sense is that nothing is wrong for you to do, nothing you do will cause you to feel guilty. The more extensive your list of things that are wrong, the more there will be for you to avoid in your effort to be free of the pain of guilt.

One symptom of living through avoidance is a hypersensitivity to what's wrong for you to do. You develop such hypersensitivity by going on a guilt trip that is arranged by someone else. Because someone else says it's wrong, you add it to the list of things you will not do. Then you feel guilty about doing them or having the urge to do them. The things we learn from our parental guidance and the things we learn from our religious teaching often are added to our personal list of dos and don'ts without examination. When you accept your moral and ethical standards without question, you essentially allow someone else to control your life. You cannot experience the satisfaction of living meaningfully if what you do or avoid doing is not your own choice but the decision of someone else.

Maybe you are willing to accept the list of right and wrong from someone else because you want to be accepted by him or her. Rejection by them would be another source of emotional pain. Because we humans are by nature societal creatures, we are susceptible to the pain that comes from rejection. Such pain can come from being excluded from a group to which you want to belong, being turned down for a job for which you have applied, getting a "no" as the result of your earnest sales pitch, or being snubbed by someone who has caught your romantic eye. The sting of rejection will always come no matter how often you expose yourself to it. You either live through avoidance of exposure to rejection, or you learn a way to relieve the pain if it occurs.

Your list of what you won't do will get longer when you are vehement about avoiding the pain of rejection. You will be compelled to restrict your vulnerability. Such restriction will interfere with your growth and development and establishing new relationships. This can have a substantial impact on your living meaningfully because growth and connection are two of the four indicators of meaningfulness. Growth and development requires your willingness to try something new and to expose yourself to the possibility of failure. You cannot form new relationships without making yourself vulnerable to rejection.

Just as physical pain serves a beneficial purpose by, for example, signaling you to rest your overworked muscles or to not touch the hot stove or to stop gorging yourself at the dinner table, emotional pain has its benefits. Guilt keeps you true to your rules of conduct. The possibility of rejection prompts you to meet appropriate societal and performance standards.

Feelings of guilt or the fear of rejection can also be a detriment to meaningful living if you allow them to be your principle motivation for doing what you do. They can cause you to miss out on opportunities that could magnify your significance. The avoidance mode of life consists of what you can't do or what you won't do because you don't want to experience the pain of guilt or rejection.

Living through avoidance will keep you wondering what might have been if you had only taken a chance.

CHAPTER 27
LIVING THROUGH PASSIVITY

*Maybe the right circumstances will come together and push
you into a place where you will do something meaningful.
And maybe not.*

Though it was many years ago and I was quite young, I remember sitting in the living room at home thinking about life. I concluded that mine was set and there was nothing I could do to shape it or alter it. I came to such conclusion based on several observations at home, school, and church.

First, I had no choice in the matter of my birth; my parents were responsible for that. I did not choose my brothers and sisters. That, too, was decided by my parents. They also decided that I would be reared in Compton.

I went to school because my mother said I had to; it was the law. Being told that it was the law led me to believe that perhaps my parents didn't have a choice about the things I thought that they decided. Maybe the law dictated the course of life. Not only did I have no say as to whether I went to school, I did not choose the classes I took. I just went, and the teacher taught whatever. I must say, however, that I liked going to school.

Listening to music on radio stations KFWB, KRLA, and KGFJ, I heard five minutes of news at the top of the hour. The news contained brief stories about what went on in Washington and Sacramento and city hall. I had no idea where those places were, so surely I had nothing to do with what went on in those distant locations.

My conclusion that I had no say in the course of my life was settled when I went to church. Attending Trinity Chapel, a congregation of the Assemblies of God denomination, I was indoctrinated with the idea that God controlled my life.

"From the foundation of the earth," I was told, "your life was predestined." "And God knows how many hairs are on your head," Sister Grace, Brother Swan, and others assured me. So what was I to conclude if I couldn't do anything to my hair without God already knowing that I was going to do it? That being so, He must have made me do it. Even through my early twenties, Sister Grace and Pastor Robinson advised me to stop looking for a wife and let God give me one. I didn't have a choice about whether I went to church. Every Sunday morning Mom pushed us toward the church, and when I got there, the church leaders warned me that I would go to hell if I forsook the assembly of myself with others. I was encouraged to memorize a portion of Hebrews 10:25 (King James Version): "Not forsaking the assembling of ourselves together, as the manner of some is..."

I began resisting the notion that someone else would determine the course of my life when I was in junior high school. I learned that the sighted students chose the classes they would take and who their teachers would be, but I didn't make such choices. In the first couple of semesters at Washington Irving Junior High School, Mrs. Boren and Mr. Bloodgood, the Braille resource teachers, decided for me. What annoyed me about their decisions was the fact that they placed my peers, Caroline and Judene, in advanced classes and put me in the lower level sections of English and history and geography. Only in seventh-grade math did I have the same class with Caroline and Judene. When I made this observation, I became obstinate and resistant. I began choosing the opposite of whatever Mrs. Boren said I ought to do. It didn't matter that her suggestion might have been good for me. I went the other way so that she wouldn't be the one deciding my junior high school life.

Is it you or is it someone else who controls the course of your life?

There are many forces that can impact the course of your life and determine your significance. The person or people responsible for your upbringing influence(s) what you do. Your parents may have made you do what you do, or it could simply be a question of what you were exposed to while you were growing up.

The place where you received your formal education has an influence on the direction of your life. The impact comes, not only from the content of the education, but it also comes from the role modeling of the instructors and the reputation of the institution.

Your religious teachings have a major influence on setting the principles by which you live, the relationships you establish, and the purpose of your life.

You may be greatly influenced by your friends. A friend can be a role model. A friend can be a source of advice and encouragement. A friend can exercise peer pressure.

What you do can also be influenced by commercial advertisements. Commercials presented in audio, visual, and print media serve to create a desire within you and then offer a way to fulfill your desire. Advertisements can also induce you to act by instilling fear of failure or rejection.

Your life might be shaped by the imaginary lives you view on television or in the movies, or about which you read in novels.

The economy can force you in one direction or another. Because you need the money, you will take the job—any job. You may also be influenced positively in that you finally venture out to start your business because you are laid off from your job.

The direction of your life can be determined by where you live and the laws and politics of your community.

So long as you are living, you cannot escape the influences of your family, education, religion, friends, commerce, economy, environment, or politics. You can, however, determine the force of the impact that these influences have on your life. You can exercise control over the direction and course of your life, or you can passively allow the forces to push you in whatever direction the circumstances favor.

❖ You are living through passivity when the depth and course of your life is determined by the circumstances or by someone other than yourself.

❖ You are living through passivity if you are working a full-time job that you hate. You do it, you say, because you need the money.

❖ You are living through passivity if you don't like your profession. You stay in it because your parents invested in your education and you don't want to disappoint them.

❖ You are living through passivity if you are doing what you do because you don't know what else to do.

❖ You are living through passivity if you don't have a job because there are no jobs in your community that fit your skills.

❖ You are living through passivity if your boss is making your life miserable, but you keep going to where he or she is.

❖ You are living through passivity if your spouse or partner is making your life miserable, but you keep silent about it.

❖ You are living through passivity if you are worried about what your friends think about what you do.

❖ You are living through passivity if you are waiting for some event to happen or waiting for enough money or waiting until the bills are paid up.

❖ You are living through passivity if you are letting your age dictate whether or not you make a career change.

❖ You are living through passivity if your disability or gender is the excuse you offer for not doing what you really want to do.

❖ You are living through passivity if you are a mature adult and you don't know what you want in life.

❖ You may be living through passivity if you are a mature adult and cannot identify your own talents and skills. This lack of self-awareness can also be the result of your being distracted by external allures.

❖ You may be living through passivity if the reason that you are reading this book is that someone suggested that you should and you could not find something else to do. However, the fact that you acted on the suggestion indicates that you are curious and searching for a greater understanding of the meaning of your life. That curiosity of yours is the force that you should allow to push you toward a life of encounter.

If you continue living through passivity, you leave the meaningfulness of your life to chance. Maybe the right circumstances will come together and push you into a place where you will do something meaningful. And maybe not.

CHAPTER 28
OVERCOMING ADVERSITY

Develop the ability to comb through the rubble of misfortune
and find the reason for hope.

I was surprised and annoyed when I was served a summons for a lawsuit for sexual harassment. I knew that Marjory had claimed that I sexually harassed her, but I thought the matter would die once found to be without merit by the personnel committee of the board of directors. Marjory had deemed it sexual harassment because I, a blind man, bumped into her while she stood in the hallway outside my office. She said I sexually harassed her when I, in handling a legal matter for her, said, "I could do more for you if you would just let me." In certain situations, these could have been harassment, but in the context of my working with Marjory, they were not. So when I saw that she was suing me for ten million dollars when my monthly gross income was fifteen hundred dollars, I thought it a joke. I called Yvonne, a lawyer friend, who smartly advised me to take the matter seriously. I called a friend who knew both Marjory and me, and she too advised that I should take the matter seriously. She believed—as I knew—that the allegations were false, but she impressed upon me that Marjory believed them to be true.

I had no sexual interest in and made no sexual advances toward Marjory. What I did was to write a negative personnel evaluation of her year and a half of work with the agency that I directed. The board asked that on my way out I evaluate the performance of all employees. After receiving Marjory's evaluation, the board instructed me to terminate her employment rather than leaving the firing to the new director. I followed the board's instruction. Marjory had expected to be hired as the new director, so being fired must have been a double blow to her.

At the time I was sued by Marjory, I was single and had been out of law school just a few years. I began to realize that depending on the outcome of the matter, my life could be permanently and adversely affected. I hired a good lawyer to represent me. The ordeal lasted three years, but in the end, the jury found in my favor.

I learned from the experience that while I can control my actions, I cannot control what others perceive of my actions or what someone else wishes to make of my actions. I also learned that if I could not overcome adverse situations, negative forces over which I had no control would beat me down.

What adversities will you overcome?

Your ability to overcome adversity is an indication that you are in control of your life. Overcoming is a life skill essential to meaningful living. Without this skill, you leave yourself vulnerable to the circumstances. When faced with circumstances over which you have no control, you can be passive and may be a victim, or you can find in the situation something meaningful to your purpose.

Adversity is a condition, situation, or set of circumstances that is unfavorable to your purpose or objectives. You could find yourself in an unfortunate situation because of something you did or a bad decision you made. You can do all the good that you know to do and face adversity because of what someone else wants from or out of you. Factors of the economy or forces of nature can put you in a bad situation. The cause does not matter. What matters is your ability to emerge from the situation with your zeal for meaningful living intact.

You can transform a situation from adversity to opportunity by searching for something favorable to your purpose. You should develop the ability to comb through the rubble of misfortune and find the reason for hope. That is, you should look for the things that will give you the confident expectation that you can still achieve your purpose, reach your goal, and live meaningfully.

To find the reason for hope, you must know what you are looking for. In what have you anchored hope? What were you building when the walls came crumbling down? Spend less time on the horror and pain of the circumstances and more time on the positive elements that can be salvaged.

When you find yourself in a situation wholly unfamiliar to you, seek counsel from someone with experience. Not just someone who faced the situation, but find someone who emerged from the situation with a list of positive outcomes. You don't need the advice of someone who will reiterate the negativity of the situation; you can do that on your own because you experience the pain directly.

You will not be able to find the reason for hope by heaping blame. Blaming yourself only increases the pain of the experience and inhibits your ability to find the opportunities that may rise from the situation. Blaming others instead of yourself can be worse. Blaming others excuses you from the responsibility of taking control of a bad situation and making it work favorably for you.

You can never overcome a difficult or an unfortunate situation by seeking revenge, retaliation, or retribution. These are retrogressive acts that magnify your own misfortune in addition to inflicting adversity on another person.

From every experience there is a lesson to be learned. You may learn how to avoid similar situations in the future. You may learn how to cope with the effects of what has happened. When you can apply the lessons learned from an adverse experience, you have overcome. This is not to say necessarily that you have conquered the situation, but you have taken control of what your life will be thereafter.

What's too hard for a man must be worth looking into.
                                        - Kenyan Proverb

PART VII:
THE COMMITMENT TO MEANINGFULNESS

Act quickly; think slowly.
 - Greek Proverb

CHAPTER 29
LIVING THROUGH ENCOUNTER

If you are not doing anything, you are not living; you are just being.

The first time I visited Las Vegas was in 1971; I went to attend a wedding. I was nineteen years old and too young to gamble, but that isn't why I didn't go to the casino. My religious upbringing instilled in my consciousness the sin of Las Vegas. With its sex-rated shows along with the gambling, my church taught me that Las Vegas was a place to avoid.

When I went to Las Vegas to attend the wedding of Jackie and Dwight, both of whom lived in Vegas, I stayed at the Westward Ho where upon check-in I was given a coupon with which I could obtain a cup of nickels—six dollars worth—in exchange for $5. I made the exchange with the help of my friends Ruth and Jack Johnson. They, with whom I traveled to Las Vegas, are the parents of my high-school friend Vykee. Ruth asked if I were going to the casino to gamble with my nickels. I responded, "No, I have a dollar more than I came with and I am going to quit while I'm ahead."

My second visit to Las Vegas was eleven years after my first. This time I took a bus trip with a group of about fifty others expressly for the purpose of trying our luck at the slot machines. By then, being almost thirty years old, I had contemplated and dismissed the gambling prohibitions taught at my church. I was greatly influenced by the biblical passage in Mark 7:15, "There is nothing from without a man, that entering into him can defile him: but the things which come out of him, those are they that defile the man." My heart was set on playing. I was intrigued by the prospect of depositing into the slot machine one dollar and getting back thousands. It didn't happen and has not happened the dozens of times I have since visited casinos in Nevada—Las Vegas, Laughlin, Mesquite, Reno, and Topaz Lake; Atlantic City, New Jersey; Council Bluffs, Iowa; Albuquerque, New Mexico; and a town outside of Johannesburg in South Africa.

During my 1982 trip to Las Vegas, Verdell, the organizer of the bus trip, turned me on to Keno. This has become my game of choice. I make trips to casinos strictly for the purpose of playing the Keno machines. I don't do so to gain a gambling windfall, but for the pleasure of playing.

Are you going for what you want?

You probably don't need the results of an academic study or a commercial survey to know that if your life is to be meaningful, it must be pleasurable. You must find pleasure that is more than what you get from watching a movie, playing a game, eating a bowl of ice cream, or spending romantic time with a partner. These are temporary points of pleasure that depend on person, place, and time. They satisfy physical drives and stimulate good feelings, but do little for the soul. If you fill your life with these temporal moments of pleasure, life may be hedonistic but will probably not be meaningful.

The pleasure that makes life meaningful is that which satisfies all three of your life's dimensions—body, mind, and soul. When you reach the third dimension—that of the soul—the joy that you get will not depend on good weather or fine company. No matter the circumstances, you are pleased.

Living through encounter is action that seeks those activities and relationships that please the soul. It is choosing from life's smorgasbord of activities the endeavors that allow you to engage your soul. It is encountering challenges. It is seeking new experiences. Living through encounter is the mode of life that is guided by the goals of expanding the mind and opening the soul.

If you are to live through encounter, you must take charge of and hold yourself responsible for your life. Taking charge and holding responsibility requires a vision, desire, talents and skills, and action.

First, you must have a vision of what you want your life to be. You should not let your vision of life be created by someone else—not your parents, not the religious leader, and not your peers. These people may add input for your consideration, but your vision must be your own creation. Your vision becomes the context of your desires, the assessment of your abilities, and your decisions of the actions you will take. You cannot satisfy your soul if your desires, abilities, and actions are in the context of the life of someone else.

Second, you must know what you want from your life experiences. Only you know and can say what your desires are. They come from within and cannot be observed from an external viewpoint. You might search yourself through contemplation and reflection or you might identify your desires through conversation and counseling.

Third, you must assess your talents and skills. Your talents are those abilities for which you have a natural expertise. Your skills are the things you learn to do. For example, you might use your talent for music as the basis for your learning to be a piano tuner. Your talent for organization may lead you to developing the skill of an events planner. A complete assessment of your talents and skills require you to continually seek new experiences. Talents and skills are best discovered from doing. You will never discover your talent for or develop your skills in personal counseling, for example, simply by sitting in a quiet place and contemplating. By engaging in the activity, you learn your prowess or weakness in the area.

Fourth, you must take action. What life will be for you depends on what you do in life. It is not a question of your vocation. Your job or profession is only the means by which you make money and acquire possessions. The scope, depth, and shape of your life depends on what you do to create your vision, what you do to fulfill your desires, and what you do to discover your talents and develop your skills. If you are not doing anything, you are not living; you are just being.

Your body is strengthened with activity. Your mind is expanded by knowledge. Your soul is opened through love. Living through encounter is the mode of life where you willingly seek out life's situations that allow you to do ALL at once—Act, Learn, and Love.

CHAPTER 30
BEING A HUMAN DOING

Living is more than being. It requires doing.

I didn't go to law school because I wanted to; I went because I had to. Graduating from law school was a prerequisite to becoming a lawyer, and I wanted to be a lawyer.

In the early weeks of my senior year at Yale in 1973, my classmates and I discussed what we would be doing after graduation. I really was uncertain about what to do. I didn't have much imagination about how to use the bachelor's degree in math that I was about to acquire. The only thing I could think of was teaching, and I didn't want to be a teacher. After I received the acceptance letter from Yale, I created an audacious plan for math studies—a bachelor's degree from Yale, a master's degree from Harvard, and a doctorate from the Massachusetts Institute of Technology. After four years of studying, however, further math studies lacked appeal to me. While mathematics stimulated my mind, it did not touch my soul.

Most of my classmates with whom I spoke planned on going to law school or medical school. Since I reasoned that a person would let me argue a case in court for them before they would let me operate on them, I decided to be a lawyer. Advice from my good friend, Harvey, influenced my decision.

My heart did not embrace the idea of going to law school as much as my head had. Consequently, I did not have much enthusiasm for submitting applications for admission to law school. I applied to only four—Yale, Stanford, University of California at Berkeley, and University of Southern California. When I told this to a classmate, he chided me for applying to so few. He confided that he applied to seventeen law schools and had already been rejected from four. My thought was that I would figure out something else to do if I got rejected from four. I didn't have to come up with an alternative because I was accepted by two of the four law schools to which I had applied.

What are you doing, and why are you doing it?

We are humans doing. From our first day to our last we are doing something—that is, we are physically engaged in some activity. Even when we sleep, we are doing something—sleeping. When you are awake but the body is still, your senses continue to perceive your environment.

You came into being when the Creative Force inspired the union of your body, mind, and soul. You impact the universe physically by what you do with your body. The function of your mind is to create thoughts and ideas and to choose actions. Your soul provides the will to act and connects what you do to the world outside you. Everything that you do involves a choice of action based on some idea initiated by your will to act. Having an impact on and being connected with the universe are not the same. Simply acting impacts. To be connected with the universe, you must act with the intent to enhance, better, or strengthen others and/or your environment. The meaningfulness of your being derives from what you are doing with your inspired union to enhance the universe.

The things that you are doing fall into three categories—things you need to do, things you have to do, and things you want to do. The things you need to do are dictated by the body's instinct for survival. What you have to do is an intellectual determination. The things you want to do emanate from your soul.

Many of the day-to-day things that we do are done because we need to. They are for physical survival. You eat and drink to obtain nourishment for the health of your body. Also, for your body's health and strength, you need to expel waste and toxins, you need to rest and sleep, and you need to exercise. To protect your body from disease and injury, you need to wash, clean, and dress it.

The things you have to do are those things that you have determined through intellectual analysis are mandated by law, norms, or prerequisites to some opportunity or benefit. They are not needed for personal survival but are secondary to the things that you want. For example, if you want to retain your liberty and freedom from incarceration, you have to obey the laws of the land. If you want to be a doctor, you have to receive medical training. If you want to attend a particular college, you have to complete and submit its application.

If you are not doing something because you need to or because you have to, you are doing it because you want to. That is to say, you are not doing it for personal survival and you are not required to do it in order to get something else. You have the option to do it or not do it without jeopardizing your health and well being.

The things you do to satisfy the needs of the mind and/or soul, you do because you want to do them. Increasing one's knowledge and engaging in intellectual exercises to improve mental functioning is a matter of choice. It is not necessary to do so to prolong life. Likewise, acting to develop and maintain spiritual well-being is something one does by choice.

Because the choice is yours, knowing the reason that you make that choice is important. Becoming aware of why you choose to do one thing or another leads to the understanding of the meaningfulness of what you do.

Here are several objectives that may dictate your wants:

A. Money or other material possessions.
B. Pleasure.

C. Power, position, or status.
D. Acceptance, approval, or recognition.
E. Happiness.
F. Revenge, retaliation, or retribution.
G. Promotion of a cause.
H. Spiritual fulfillment.
I. Growth and development.
J. Establishing or nurturing relationships.
K. Religious obeisance.

If this list does not identify all the reasons you choose to do one thing or another, add to the list. Once you have a comprehensive list of objectives, you can use the list to identify the benefits that you get from each of the activities in which you are involved. You can derive multiple benefits from a single activity. For example, you may coach your daughter's softball team because it (D) gets you recognition in the community, (E) makes you happy, and (J) nurtures your relationship with your child.

To make each moment of your life meaningful, you must be aware of the benefits that you are seeking and getting from each of the things you do. If the benefit is meaningful to you, then the time spent on it is time meaningfully spent. Conversely, if you are not deriving a meaningful gain from what you do, you are wasting life. Your health and well-being, which are meaningful, are the benefits you derive from things you need to do (as discussed above—eating, exercising, resting, etc.). The time you give to have-to activities is time meaningfully spent if the have-to activity is the prerequisite for a meaningful activity or benefit. Finally, for all of your want-to activities, you should identify your reasons for participating from your comprehensive objectives list. There are two different ways you can conduct this analysis:

1. Ask: With regard to my doing ____ (activity), am I getting ____ (substitute each item from the objectives list)? Example: With regard to my attending the Toastmasters convention, am I having fun (Item B)? Those items that receive a yes answer are the benefits from the activity.

2. Ask: If I didn't get ____ (item from the list), would I continue doing ____ (specific activity)? Example: If I didn't get spiritual fulfillment (Item H), would I continue working on my present job? A no answer means that spiritual fulfillment is a benefit you are getting from your job. If the answer is yes, then getting spiritual fulfillment is not important to your employment.

After you have identified all of the objectives for your activities, you can then ask: Are these objectives meaningful? You can then determine how much of your life you are devoting to what is meaningful.

Once you conduct your analysis, if you discover that most of your life is devoted to doing things that have little meaning for you, you will have identified the problem with satisfying the yearning to be significant, to make a difference, or to leave the world as a better place. This discovery, however, can be the steppingstone to the path that leads you to making each moment meaningful. Your goal should be to increase the amount of time you spend doing things that you want to do that have meaningful objectives.

You can increase the meaningfulness of your need-to-do and have-to-do activities by doing them in conjunction with a want-to-do activity that has a meaningful benefit. The ideal employment, for example, would be the one that provides spiritual fulfillment and an income to meet your needs. You need to eat. When you have dinner with a friend, you make eating not just a necessary activity, but also a meaningful activity by simultaneously nurturing your friendship. You may have to go to law school to be an attorney, but you can make law school meaningful by volunteering at a legal aid clinic to represent indigent clients.

Living is more than being. It requires doing. If the things that you are doing do not give you benefits that you consider meaningful, then your living is insignificant. Whether your life is significant or insignificant is your choice because you choose to do what you are doing.

CHAPTER 31
KNOWING WHAT YOU WANT

Knowing what you want means understanding what void or longing underlies your desire and the circumstances or actions it would take to meet the need or fill the void.

Jaci and I were in the market for a new minivan. Having owned a Plymouth Voyager for thirteen years and having a family of four children, we identified the Chrysler Town & Country as our move up. We wanted to do some price comparisons. One Saturday afternoon, while traveling through Carson, California (about ninety miles from home), we decided to stop in at a Chrysler dealership.

As soon as Jaci and I got out of the car and closed the doors, a saleswoman pounced on us and asked if she could help us. She wanted to know what we were looking for—what type of vehicle we wanted. We told her our preference.

After we walked around the lot for a while without seeing what we wanted, the saleswoman volunteered, "I have an offer on a Plymouth Voyager you won't be able to refuse."

I bit. We had been happy with our Plymouth Voyager. If she had such an offer, I'd be willing to modify my desire for a Town & Country.

As the saleswoman drove up with her compelling offer, Jaci commented to me disappointedly, "I see a problem already. It's purple."

My thought was, "If the offer is good enough, we'll paint it."

Following the test drive, the saleswoman led Jaci and me into her office, a space just large enough for a desk, three chairs, and the three of us. Pulling a form from her desk drawer, the saleswoman began asking Jaci questions to complete an application, starting with her Social Security and driver's license numbers. When she got to the question of her employment, Jaci told her that she did not work. In a tone of curiosity and confusion, the saleswoman asked, "How do you expect to buy a car if you don't have a job?"

Jaci responded, "Because my husband works."

"Then we need his information," the sales woman snapped as she ripped up the form she had begun and pulled a fresh one from the drawer. She then directed her questions to me.

I refused to answer her first question, "What is your Social Security Number?" I told her that I wasn't answering any of her questions until I heard the offer that I wouldn't be able to refuse. I challenged her insistence that she needed to run a credit check before she could make the offer.

The saleswoman elicited the help of the sales manager. Standing in the doorway, he asked what the problem was. I recounted our search for a Town & Country and the saleswoman's declaration that she had an offer I couldn't refuse on a Voyager. He scolded the saleswoman for trying to sell me something I didn't want. He asked for my indulgence for two more minutes while the saleswoman went to retrieve the Town & Country. I set the timer on my talking watch. Jaci and I left the dealership when the watch announced that two minutes had elapsed.

Do you know what you want?

To make the best choices for yourself and to avoid distractions, you must know what you want. To know where to go to get what you want, you have to know what you want. To keep from being led or pushed down a path where you don't want to go, you must know what you want.

Knowing what you want is being aware and conscious of your needs and desires that prompt your actions and dictate your choices. In the context of this awareness and consciousness, your needs and desires are both considered.

The consideration is not whether they are mandatory or optional, but the extent to which they compel you to act.

Needs are the urges that drive you to sustain life. To the extent that you need to continue living, you should be aware of them as you try to determine your wants.

Desire is an impulse to fill a void. It is a call to act on a drive, follow an urge, or respond to a longing. Your desire stimulates your mind to consider thoughts of what would satisfy you. Knowing what you want means understanding what void or longing underlies the desire and the circumstances or actions it would take to meet the need or fill the void. You can have a drive, say, to make money and may do it well, but acting on that drive and making lots of money may not fill the void you feel. If your underlying longing is for something that money cannot buy, no amount of money made will fill the void. What you do to obtain satisfaction must match the desire in order for you to obtain satisfaction.

Have you ever responded "I don't know" to the question, What do you want? If so, you have acknowledged that you have desires but don't fully understand them. The question is not whether or not you want something; it is whether or not you know what you want. Only you can answer the question. If you seek advice from friends or family, they will tell you what they imagine you want. In truth, their advice or suggestions will be what they want.

Set aside an hour today, or plan to do it within the next week, to engage your thoughts and confront your feelings as you answer this question: What do I want? Use the following guidelines to help you answer:

Do it yourself. Find a place and time where and when no one else is around. The only input you should have is from your thoughts and your emotions. Silence is better, but if you must have music, choose music without words. Let your music be soft enough that it doesn't drown out your thoughts.

What to do. Using whatever writing method is best for you, write "I want ___" twenty-five times. Fill in the blanks with briefly worded items—one to five words. Resist the temptation to write explanations for your wants. For example, you might write "money" and not "money so I can pay off my bills." In the next chapter, we will discuss the reasons for your wants. Fill in as many of the twenty-five blanks as you can. You don't have to stop at twenty-five. If you have more than twenty-five, write them down.

No editing. Let this session be a time for brainstorming. Write down whatever comes to your mind or your heart. Don't filter your thoughts in any way. Your list of wants need not be worded correctly. You shouldn't concern yourself with whether or not they can be achieved. Don't worry about how they might be perceived by others.

Record your list. Use the method that is best for you to make a tangible record—pen and paper, audio recording, electronic data file. Keeping a record of your desires is important for four reasons. First, the memory is fleeting and you are likely to forget them. You must be able to refer to them later, and you don't want to have to re-create the list. Second, your desires change based on circumstances, so you must be able to capture them at a particular point in time and to recognize when a change occurs. Third, when your desires are written, it is easier to take them one by one and figure out how each can be satisfied. Fourth, the recording of your wants is the first act to bringing them about.

Let it age or settle. When you have completed your list, set it aside. You should go back to it only if you think of something to add. Let it sit for several hours or a day or even a week, so that when you return to it for review, you do so with a refreshed perspective.

Knowledge is like a garden: If it is not cultivated, it cannot be harvested.

- African Proverb

CHAPTER 32
KNOWING WHY YOU WANT IT

*Knowing why you want what you want gives you a
consciousness that can serve as your guide for choosing what
you will do with your life.*

One Thursday evening, I lay on my bed crying in my
pillow and wishing that I were not blind. It was in 1980. It
was the night before my first appearance in court as a lawyer.
It would be for a preliminary hearing for my client, a friend's
brother, who had been charged with five counts of armed
robbery. I needed to go to the law library to do some
research, but I couldn't find anyone who could assist me with
driving and reading. As I lay enveloped in my self-pity, the
hour grew late and the library closed. I had to be in court,
eighty-five miles away, at nine o'clock Friday morning. I
would have to do the best that I could with what I could
remember from law school.

This was the second of only two times in my life that I
wished that I could see—a wish toward which I could do
nothing to make come true. The first time occurred about
twelve years earlier when I was in high school. Giving advice
to us guys about how to treat a lady, my Spanish teacher said,
"If you want to know what a lady is thinking, look into her
eyes." There was a lady whose thoughts I wanted to learn.

I have not wished for sight since that pitiful Thursday
night. I came to realize that sight was not what I really
wanted. I wanted independence. I wanted the ability to do
what I wanted without the help of someone else. Well, no,
that isn't what I wanted either. People are important to me,
and my relationships with them are valuable. What I really
wanted was to have the assistance I needed when I needed it.
This, I realized, was something I could do something about

and bring into fruition through my own efforts. I could get what I wanted notwithstanding my blindness.

I was able to figure out what I really wanted and how I might get it by asking myself the tough question, Why? Actually, the question is easy to ask; the answers can be tough to reach or tough to accept.

Why do you want what you want?

Although having a list of wants and desires is essential, for leading a meaningful life, knowing what you want involves a lot more than a tangible list of your needs and desires. Knowing what you want requires awareness and consciousness. For your awareness of your wants to be meaningful, you must be conscious of what underlies each want that you have identified. An unconscious pursuit of your desires can take you down unintended paths and can result in a dissatisfying life.

(If you have not yet made your list of wants, refer to the previous chapter on "Knowing What You Want" before continuing this chapter.)

Consciousness of your wants is gained by asking: Why? Asking why is an effective tool for peeling away layers of insignificance, for dissecting excuses, for breaking mindless habits, and for uncovering the motivation for what you do.

The answer to "Why?" can help you get to the heart of your desires. You may learn, for example, that it is not more money that you want, but rather freedom from worry about how your basic living needs will be met. Having more money is just the method you have devised for getting the freedom you desire. Once you are conscious of the fact that freedom from worry is what you want, not more money, you can then identify other ways to obtain the freedom you desire without getting a second job or a higher paying job. You might decide to reduce your expenses to eliminate your worry.

Sharing an apartment with a friend instead of living alone might be the better option.

The answer to "Why?" can help you distinguish between what you want and what you believe are the expectations of others. You may learn, for example, that you want to be a dancer, but your family expects you to get a more stable job. When you are conscious of the fact that you are living to please others rather than yourself, you will be able to make the decisions that fulfill your desires instead of fulfilling the desires of others. You will never satisfy the yearning to be significant by fulfilling some other person's wishes while ignoring your own.

The answer to "Why?" can help you discover what motivates you. To be motivated is to have a compelling reason to do what you know you can and ought to do. You may learn, for example, that you like being the focus of attention and that drives you to being an actress. Being conscious of why you do what you do is a necessary element of self-motivation. It will be the antidote to discouragement and disappointment if and when they arise.

Answering "Why?" can also help you to identify the method for getting what you want. You may learn, for example, that you can fulfill your desire to improve your interviewing skills by taking a class at the community college. However, the college class may not be the thing to do if the job interview for which you want the enhanced skills is before the class ends. Private coaching may be the option for getting what you want. The path to what you want can be mapped out only when you are conscious of why you want what you do.

Review your list of wants that you created from the previous chapter. One by one, consider each item on your list. Ask yourself: Why do I want this? Write the answer down. It may indicate a replacement for the item that you are analyzing because you have peeled off a layer to the heart of what you want. If the answer reveals that the listed item is not what you want at all but rather what someone else wants, it would indicate that you should remove the item from your list. Answering the "Why?" question for each item you analyze may also help you define what "meaningful" means to you. Stay on a single item and keep asking why as you peel off layers of information. Ask until you have reached the heart of the matter—that is, until you get to an answer such as "It serves my purpose in life," "It is what I believe," "It is what is meaningful to me." You can then move on to the next item on your list.

When you have given consideration to all your wants and understand why you want them, you will have an awareness and consciousness about what you are looking for in life that can serve as your guide for making decisions and choosing what you will do with your life.

CHAPTER 33
GETTING WHAT YOU WANT

*Action makes the difference between getting what you want
and receiving what you want.*

I was at my brother Joe's house with most of my siblings after the memorial service for Joe's wife. During a lull in the conversation—a lull that rarely occurs when my family gets together, my sister, Dolly, spoke, "Little Brother, you've got a big birthday coming up. What are you going to do?"

"Nothing special," I answered. "I have no plans."

"Are you going to have a party?" she probed.

"Nope," I replied.

My sister, Jessie, chimed in, "How do you know? Jaci may want to give you a fiftieth birthday party."

"She hasn't said anything about a birthday party," I answered with certainty.

"It may be a surprise," Dolly suggested.

"Nope, she wouldn't do that. I don't like surprises."

"But what if she wants to give you a surprise party?" Dolly pressed.

My response closed the discussion. "I don't like surprises. I don't want a surprise birthday party. If you told me that you didn't like a particular kind of perfume, should I buy that perfume for you just because I like it? I am sure Jaci is not going to give me a surprise birthday party because she knows I don't like surprises."

I don't like surprises because they give me a sense of being not in control. This is not to say that I have not been surprised from time to time and enjoyed what I received. But I'd rather be an influence over what I get and what happens to me.

Are you getting what you want, or are you just receiving what you want?

As it relates to meaningful living, the key to getting what you want is control. You must be able to characterize your wants in terms of objectives over which you have control. That is, when you develop your list of I-wants and edit and revise your list with the probing "Why" question, the end product should be a list of things that you can obtain through your own efforts. If they are not—if they are things left up to circumstances and chance, the only thing that you can do is to sit and wait and see if they happen. You may want to win the state lottery. The only thing you can do is buy a $1 ticket and wait. Nothing else you do can ensure that you will be the lucky one out of forty-three million. Well, okay, you can ensure your win by purchasing forty-three million different number combinations. But if you had the forty-three million dollars needed to do that, to win the lottery probably wouldn't be one of your wishes.

Here are the things over which you have complete control: Knowledge, Hope, Will, Action, Reaction, and Determination. These are your characteristics and qualities that will determine whether or not you get what you want. No, they do not guarantee your success at getting what you want. They do, however, maximize the influence or control that you can exercise over any situation in which you find yourself and optimize your benefit from such situation.

The Knowledge that controls the outcome (and income) you seek—which I will call "action knowledge"—is broader than that obtained through formal education and/or training. You must know when formal education and training are necessary or beneficial. You must know what you want. You should know why you want it. In addition, action knowledge includes knowing the location of what you want, knowing who has it and whether they are willing to give it up, knowing what you need to do to get it, and knowing when you should go after it. Action knowledge also requires that you know when you should alter your approach or abandon the endeavor.

For action knowledge to be an element that allows you to maintain control over what you get, it must be knowledge that you have obtained personally or that you have verified when it comes through someone else. You must know that the source is reliable, and you must know the difference between fact, opinion, and conjecture.

When you possess action knowledge, you have a basis for hope. Hope comes from within you. You are, therefore, in control. Hope is not a tangible object that some other person can give to or take from you. External factors such as the state of the economy, a doctor's prognosis, or other circumstances in which you find yourself are simply the places from which you find a reason to hope. Hope provides you the impetus to make the best of what appears to be a bad situation.

Will is the strength of your being. It is the power of the soul that drives your actions. Your will is ignited by desire and fueled by hope. It doesn't take much will to obtain that which is easy to reach. A marathon runner need not summon the force of will to finish the first mile; she will summon the strength of will for the last, however. Will is the power to meet the challenges in life with courage. Acting with great courage in the midst of uncertainty can get you just as much as acting on high probability. Will is the strength to act whatever the situation.

Getting what you want is still left up to chance even when you have Knowledge, Hope, and Will unless these three factors are manifested through Action. Action makes the difference between getting what you want and receiving what you want. The latter is merely a matter of chance. When you are willing to take action, you can get results that past history and conventional thinking indicate are not supposed to happen.

Your Reactions to situations also matter. There are two different situations you can find yourself in—that which favors your getting what you want and that which is adverse to what you want. The only way for you to know which is which is for you to take the first step and ascertain what resistance is present. With no resistance, you can continue to act and take the next step. When you encounter resistance, you must react in the direction of your goal. If, for example, you want to be a published novelist, the first step is to write. You are not likely to encounter resistance to writing other than the occasional writer's block. You still write. On the other hand, your efforts to find an agent to represent you might prompt you to abandon the initial goal to be a novelist. Your reaction to such challenge should not be to quit but rather to find an alternative for getting published.

Your ability to react again and again when the circumstances are not working in your favor is Determination. When you are determined to get what you want, you possess the capacity to return to the first stage of the process—that is, Knowledge. You can increase your fund of knowledge and thereby alter Hope, Will, Action, and Reaction. With the knowledge you gain from your prior experience, you can determine what changes you must make to your approach and in your actions that will achieve your goal. The additional knowledge might even prompt you to modify your goals.

Getting what you want requires that you act on your own behalf. What you obtain is the result of what you do. It is possible for you to receive something that you want without acting in your best interest, but waiting for chance will not allow you to make each moment of your life meaningful. When you wait for life to happen, there are likely to be many wasted moments of inaction. Inaction can never satisfy the yearning to be significant because you were created to be a human doing.

CHAPTER 34
CREATING THE MEMORIES

*You are responsible for what you do and for what you want
to be remembered.*

One morning, I woke up to the headlines on "Morning Edition" of National Public Radio that it was the fortieth anniversary of the death of Martin Luther King Jr. Steve noted that Dr. King has now been dead longer than he lived; he died when he was thirty-nine years old. I heard members of the Memphis Sanitation Union recount King's involvement in their workers' strike. I heard a couple retell their emotional reactions to King's "I've Been to the Mountaintop" speech. All the comments throughout the day were about how people were made to feel when listening to one of Dr. King's speeches.

With this recounting of the life of Martin Luther King Jr. on my mind, I headed out the door on my way to catch the bus that would take me seventy-five miles to my office in downtown Los Angeles. It being a Friday, the driver made good time on the 14, 210, and 2 Freeways. But then we got caught up in traffic because streets were blocked off downtown—closed because there was a large funeral procession for a firefighter who had been killed a week earlier in the line of duty. Fellow firefighters, law enforcement officers, and public officials as well as friends and family members were gathering to show their respects and to celebrate the life of a man.

It was unusual for me to be traveling to my office on a Friday. But there I was on my way, not to go to work, but to rendezvous with my mother and nephew to attend the funeral service of a close family friend, Michael Gibbs.

As young boys, Michael and I played together. We drew circles in the ground and got down on our knees to play marbles. We straddled broomsticks as our horses as we played cowboys and Indians. We did household chores together; we went to church together. After we graduated from high school and matured as adults, the paths of our lives diverged. They came together again when we both moved to the Antelope Valley in north Los Angeles County, but we would not spend time together as adults like we did as children. I had the chance to visit Michael in the hospital days before his death, and he seemed to be doing quite well. In fact, he was discharged two days after my visit. But two days after his discharge, he was admitted into intensive care. I spent a few minutes at his bedside a couple of hours before he died.

I shared these experiences when I spoke at Michael's funeral service, and I encouraged his friends, family, and other relatives to cherish the memories. Others spoke about what they would remember about Michael's life.

What memories are you creating to be shared?

You may view life on a time continuum that stretches from the time of your birth to the instant of your death. This span of time includes past, present, and future. The present isn't very long. It is but an instant, and then suddenly it is the past. The present is just the conversion point of past and future. The future exists only as a hope and an expectation.

Pause a minute before reading the next sentence to consider your life. What did you just think about? The likelihood is that your response to that command was to invoke the past and your recall of what your life has been up to now. Your consideration of life relies on your memory of the past.

Life is mostly memories with an instant to create them. The instant to create life's memories is now. Once the present instant is passed, it is added to your treasure chest of memories.

You can lay no claim to tomorrow until it becomes now. Once it is now, it becomes yours to do what you will with it, but you must act with urgency. In an instant, what you do now is just a memory to make room for the next moment to which you lay claim.

When we die, we lose the ability to claim the future and, thereby, to create and share with others new memories. Life becomes a fixed and finite set of memories to be cherished by those with whom we created them.

You can create your memories by first creating a mental image of what you want your memories to be. That image then becomes the mold with which you shape the things you do now. You can create memories that highlight things, places, people, achievements, impact, emotions, and so on.

If, for example, you want to create memories of what you have achieved, then the things you do now will stress goal setting, attaining, and resetting. Once you accomplish your goal, you can check off the box of achievement, hang the award certificate, or mount the trophy. Then you move to the next goal. Those who remember you will remember the things you accomplished.

If you want to create memories of what you have amassed, then the things you do now will focus on accumulating possessions. Your awards become statements of how much money you have amassed. Your trophies might be houses, cars, art, jewelry, or businesses. You will be remembered for what you left behind for friends, family, or other beneficiaries to divide and share.

If you want to create memories of what impact you have had on the lives of others, then people have to be the center of the things you do now. The relationships you form will hold priority over the things you get or the recognition you earn. When people gather to remember your time on earth, they will share how you impacted their lives.

There is no limit to the memories you can create. How you are remembered will depend on what you do, for whom you do it, and your motivation for doing it. What you are remembered for will vary based on the stage of your life at which another person looks. Those who look at your life as a young adult may remember you for your achievements. Those who see your life at a later stage might remember your service to others. You cannot be responsible for how another person perceives what you do and your motive for doing it, but you are responsible for what you do and for what you want to be remembered.

CHAPTER 35
CREATING A PATH TO FULFILLMENT

Holding on to things can keep you from moving to a place
where your life would be more meaningful.

I came to the realization that TV-watching can be a life-consuming habit even for a blind man. At a time when things were going well for me—I was married with two children, owned a house, and had a well-paying, prestigious job—I found myself spending an average of three hours a night in front of the television. One hour was spent on news—a half an hour for local events and a half an hour on national news. The other two hours were for game shows. I watched *Tic-Tac-Dough*. I watched *Jeopardy!* I watched *Wheel of Fortune*. I watched *The $10,000 Pyramid*. Each show was for thirty minutes.

One day I did the simple calculation: If I watch TV an average of 3 hours a day, then one-eighth of my life would be watching television. If I live to be 72 years old, then 9 full years of my life would be spent in front of the TV.

After figuring this out, I considered what could be accomplished in nine years. I got a bachelor's degree in math from Yale and a law degree from U.S.C. and I passed the California bar exam within nine years. It wasn't even a full nine years. I had summer, spring, and holiday breaks.

The recognition of what I would be foregoing by watching TV prompted me to turn it off. I still watch TV, but I make certain that the time spent contributes to fulfilling my purpose, promoting my growth, and nurturing beneficial relationships without compromising my principles and beliefs.

Are you spending the majority of your life on the things that matter most to you?

By the time you began reading this book, you were already living—or life was already happening to you. Your life is already a complex of obligations, activities, relationships, and stuff. If you are not fulfilled by what you have and what you are doing, you must create a path that will lead to fulfillment. Looking at where you are now, you are challenged with the task of determining what of your life is meaningful and what is not. Then you must begin shedding that which is not. Some of your work to create a path to fulfillment will be easy; sometimes it will be difficult to let go.

You can begin creating a path by tracking what you do for a week and identifying whether the activity fulfills your purpose, promotes your growth and personal development, and/or nurtures beneficial relationships. Follow these guidelines:

❖ Be certain that the seven-day period you track is a typical week for you. You want to be sure to analyze the activities that usually occupy your time.

❖ Record the time you spend on each activity, including eating, sleeping, personal hygiene and grooming, house cleaning, running errands, commuting, playing, exercising, etc. To facilitate the tracking of time, you may wish to round the time to the nearest hour, half hour, or quarter hour. Do what's easiest for you.

❖ Place each activity for the week in one of four categories—Purpose, Growth, Relationships, and Waste. If the activity can go into more than one category, treat the list of categories as a priority ranking and put the activity in the highest category to which it applies.

❖ Once you have completed the analysis for your typical week, apply the evaluation (Steps 1 to 3) to other activities that did not get included in your seven-day review. You should include things you do regularly but less often than weekly. For example, include activities that you do monthly, annually, etc. that weren't captured in your seven-day review.

If your tracking reveals that you are spending any time on meaningless activities—i.e., Waste, then your path clearing should begin with eliminating the Waste. You should immediately develop a plan for stopping the wasteful activity. If you can, stop immediately. Every moment you continue with waste is wasted life. If you have an obligation to complete a term of service or project, do so with a plan to not renew your obligation. Perhaps you can transfer the obligation to another person for whom it would be a meaningful activity.

Once you have identified the things that you do that are not contributing to your growth, beneficial relationships, and purpose, you should find it easier to say "no" to commitments that are not meaningful opportunities for you.

If your week-long tracking reveals that no time is wasted but rather all of your time is spent on the meaningful activities of purpose, growth, and beneficial relationships, then creating the path to fulfillment will entail a plan to maximize the time spent on purpose. The goal is to reach the point that your growth and development, your relationships, and your self-definition are all connected to purposeful living. The more time you spend on activities that fulfill your purpose, the more you will experience the satisfaction of fulfilling your yearning for significance. Second to purpose is self-development. You should spend more time on the health of your body, mind, and soul before you focus on nurturing relationships. If you are doing the right things toward fulfilling your purpose and taking care of yourself, activities that allow you to establish and nurture beneficial relationships will follow naturally.

Creating a path to fulfillment also requires an evaluation of the value of the relationships in which you are involved. You can begin by identifying the people with whom you interact in your seven-day tracking of activities. Add to the list those relationships that involve less than weekly interactions. For your life to be meaningful, you should get rid of relationships from which you derive no meaningful benefit—that is, they do not serve to fulfill your purpose or to promote your growth. These can be relationships that you maintain out of a sense of obligation, relationships that cause you pain, and relationships that simply waste your time. Those people who are involved in your purposeful living and your self-development are the people with whom you want to spend time. If you are maintaining a relationship out of a sense of obligation, you should work on meeting your obligation in the least amount of time. Every moment you spend in a relationship that you don't want to be in is a moment without meaning.

If a relationship is causing you pain, you have three options—remove the source of the pain, end the relationship, or suffer. If you choose the latter, you have only yourself to blame. There may be pain in terminating a relationship, but once it is ended, healing can begin. Healing can never occur if the source of the hurt is not addressed.

The simplest way to terminate relationships that are time wasters is to avoid the time-wasting activity. If you have a relationship with a person who lures you into the time-wasting activity, learn to say "no." If you are the lure, lead both you and the person into meaningful activities.

Some meaningful things can be overdone. The path that you create to fulfillment may require that you cut down on the amount of time you spend on certain activities. For example, eating, sleeping, and exercising are meaningful for a healthy body, but you can overeat, sleep too much, and hurt yourself with too much exercise. Watching, listening to, or reading the news can be meaningful, but an overdose of the negativity that is dispensed can weaken your mind. It may be important for you to know that the heart of your government is still beating, but you don't have to listen to every beat.

You can also spend too much time staying in contact through the Internet, e-mail, and text messaging. The fact that you can now be connected to people around the world with ease, should not entice you into spending more time on relationships and entertainment than you spend on fulfilling purpose and growing.

The path that you create to fulfillment must include an appropriate amount of rest and recreation. You should avoid both having too little entertainment as well as having too much entertainment. Be a participant in sports, not just a spectator. Engage in recreational or entertainment activities that involve other people but do not necessarily involve spending money. In doing so, in a single activity you get recreation and strengthen relationships without increasing the need to make more money.

The path to fulfillment may require that you cut back on spending. When you reduce your need to make money, it is easier for you to quit working at a meaningless job. Here are some ways to cut your spending:

❖ Stop all the activities you identified as waste that cost you money.
❖ Consume less.
❖ Don't buy just because someone else has it.
❖ Don't buy just because a new model is out when the old model still works for you.
❖ Share expenses by renting to or from someone else or by buying together with someone else.

❖ Buy without borrowing the money—i.e., use current cash instead of credit cards.

If you find yourself buying to fill a void, try filling it with meaningfulness, not material. Material will bring temporary satisfaction; meaningfulness is for a lifetime.

The things that you own, possess, or hold can clutter the path to fulfillment because protecting, preserving, cleaning, and caring for them take time. Clear your path to fulfillment by getting rid of the things that do not serve your purpose or promote your growth. Hold a yard sale or an Internet sale to turn things that are no longer useful to you into money that you can use meaningfully. Donate stuff that you can't sell. Throw away (recycle when you can) stuff that no longer has a use to anyone. Holding on to things can keep you from moving to a place where your life would be more meaningful.

There are 168 hours in a week. If your tracking reveals that you spend fewer than 84 hours serving your purpose and developing yourself, then your work is cut out for you. Keep working to create a path to purposeful living. The time you spend creating a path itself is time meaningfully spent.

PART VIII:
THE SATISFIED LIFE

We will be known forever by the tracks we leave.
                                    - Dakota Proverb

CHAPTER 36
MAKING A DIFFERENCE

What you choose to do with your life moment to moment determines whether the difference you make will be positive or negative.

When I was first hired to do my current job as an administrative law judge, the chief of the division offered these words of advice and wisdom: "Every case that you hear and decision that you write affects someone's life." He wanted me to recognize that while I had been hired to adjudicate matters involving social services programs administered by the State of California, the impact of what I did involved the lives of the residents of the state.

After twenty-nine years of being hired, I heard and wrote decisions in nearly seventy-five hundred cases. That's the only statistic I can give you. I had no contact with a person or family after I issued the decision, so I cannot tell you how many lives have been affected and how lives have changed. I am confident, however, that I have made a difference.

A difference between what and what?...when and when?...to or for whom?

You are the difference. Without you and your contribution to your piece of the world, nothing would be the same. It is difficult, if not impossible, for you to imagine what the world would be without you, so you cannot in this present life know the difference your life has made. You can't know the extent of the impact your life has had. You will never be able to know all the lives you have touched because people you have not met are touched by what you do. People who are not yet born may be positively impacted by what you do today or what you did yesterday.

If only you could get a glimpse of the world that would have been had you not been as did the fictional character, George Bailey, in the 1946 movie, *It's a Wonderful Life*. George saw that if he had not lived, he would not have been around to save his brother from drowning. His brother, then, would not have been around to serve as a pilot in the navy to contribute to the country's victory in World War II. What a difference George made with that seemingly small act of saving his drowning brother.

You should not assess your ability to make a difference by comparing the way things are today to the way they could be or ought to be. Such comparison should be made only as a way of creating a hopeful vision of the future. You can use such view of tomorrow as the basis for your decisions on what to do today. The future should not be used to judge the value of the past. The difference that you have already made can only be measured by comparing the way things are today to what they would have been had you not lived and done what you did.

The meaningfulness of what you have done cannot be measured quantitatively. What matters is not how many people have been impacted, how much money you are able to donate, or how long you can serve, but whether the difference you made was positive. Every positive difference has its importance relative to its purpose and the sphere of impact. For example, you can only judge the importance of sunshine over rain relative to the geographic region and the need that exists at the time. Both rain and sunshine have the potential of being positive, and they both can be negative. At a time of drought, another day of sunshine may be negative. In such situation, clouds filled with rain would make a positive difference.

The difference that you make in this world cannot be measured by comparing what you do to what you see other people do. The difference you make by caring for a child with muscular dystrophy is no less significant than the difference a well-known actress makes in raising money for the Muscular Dystrophy Association. Both actions serve humanity. Both actions display the talents, skills, and/or abilities of the performer. There is no way to measure which act would have the more lasting impact. Without either, the world would not be the same.

You are the difference. What you choose to do with your life moment to moment determines whether the difference you make will be positive or negative. Whether or not your impact is positive or negative can only be known in the results of what you do—results, which you may never learn in this lifetime.

Your yearning to make a difference is most likely a yearning to see the difference and/or to be recognized for what you have done. The significant difference that you make most often cannot be seen. You may be able to see a difference if you volunteer with Habitat for Humanity. You can see a completed structure. What you may never know, however, is the impact that structure has on the lives of the people who call it home. Though you may never meet the person whose life is bettered by your act, your driving one nail in the structure makes a difference.

The problem you seek to solve need not be a global one for your efforts to be meaningful. Your small personal action can have a large impact that you may not notice or recognize until years later. For example, the impact on the world of your rearing a child will be known only after many years. Nor do you have to fix the problem to be significant. Millions of children may go to bed hungry tonight, but if you were responsible for feeding five, you made a difference.

You must develop the confidence and self-assurance that what you are doing is making a positive difference in at least one life. That assurance comes from looking at the life in which the difference can easily be measured. Yours. Are you fulfilling the purpose the universe has assigned to you? If so, you are making a difference. Are you growing and developing from the activities you choose to devote life to? If so, you are making a difference. Are you sharing your purpose and your growth through your relationships with others? If so, you are making a difference. Without your living in purpose, growing and developing, and establishing relationships with others, the world would not be the same. You've made it what it is today.

CHAPTER 37
HAVING IMPACT

You are not responsible for measuring the impact. You must trust that the forces of the universe will maximize the benefit of your contribution.

The poem that Maude Riley often recited to me (see Chapter 22) contains only twenty-five words. With the recitation of those twenty-five words, which would take only twelve seconds to speak, her life had an impact that she probably never imagined. If she thought of having an impact at all, it would have been to encourage a blind teenage boy to do his best. If that were the only effect of her words, it would be evidence of her meaningful living. But causing me to be committed to excellence with everything that I do isn't all that Maude's recitation of the poem did. Her twenty-five words have had global impact.

About three decades after listening to Maude's poem, I began including the principle of excellence in my speeches. I talk about excellence to other people with disabilities to encourage them to not let the low opinion that others have of their abilities be the standard they set for themselves. I talk about excellence to groups labeled as minorities to help them believe in the major role they play in this world. I have been hired by multinational corporations to speak on excellence in entertainment, insurance, and finance. I have addressed the matter of excellence in city, county, state, and federal government. I have presented a speech on excellence on stages in Indonesia, Malaysia, South Africa, Taiwan, and most of the states of the United States. I have memorialized the message of excellence in my book—*The Excellence Book: 104 Principles for Living and Working*—of which I have sold copies around the globe.

What impact twelve seconds of twenty-five words spoken in the privacy of one's home has had! Maude didn't donate money to a worldwide cause. She did not quit a job to devote her life to a noble calling. She didn't have a household name to lend to a cause. She simply recited twenty-five words to a neighbor to have an impact on the world in which she lives.

How are you having an impact?

For your life to have impact does not require money, special abilities, educational degree, position of authority, fame, notoriety, or lots of time. You have an impact on others, on society, and/or on the world, when you do something that becomes a factor in the meaningful living of someone else.

Having impact on the world requires only that you have an impact on one person. What you do for that one individual to make his or her life meaningful starts a ripple that can emanate globally. Your one beneficiary may do something that impacts one more person or maybe one million people. The number of people touched by this ripple effect is not the measure of impact. The precise number can never be known, and you should not spend any time trying to ascertain it.

You may never know the one person whose life you have impacted because anything you do can be impactful. Your dancing on stage in front of an audience whom you never meet can have an impact on someone. The person watching you crochet as you wait in the doctor's office can be impacted by what you do. The person who overhears you thanking the teller for patiently handling your bank transaction can be impacted.

The impact that you have can come, not only from those things that you do with the purpose to have an impact, but also from things you do and say that you never imagined would be impactful. You may intend to have an impact by volunteering your medical services to victims of an earthquake, and your smile as you work may have more of an impact than the stitches you placed to treat the wound. You might write a speech to help battered women free themselves from their attacker, and the life of one person in the audience may be changed from your throw-away line (a line not related to the subject of abuse) about the importance of staying in contact with your children.

The ripple effect from what you do can go on forever. It can begin with small ripples that grow into large waves. It can begin with large waves that diminish in size but remain constantly in motion. It can have a tsunami effect—that is, begin in one place with no evidence of effect and later explode with impact halfway around the globe. In your lifetime, you will never know the breadth of the influence that your impact has.

In the context of meaningful living, impact is by definition to be a positive factor in the life of another person. You may do something that has a negative influence on another individual. If you do it intentionally, you are being destructive and will not experience the satisfaction of fulfilling the yearning to be significant. The yearning for significance can only be satisfied with intentions that give and serve to edify. If there is a negative result from what you do that you did not intend, you need not feel responsible for the result. So long as you acted in accordance with your purpose and intended good, the universe will provide the resolution of the unintended negativity.

Because you may not know who is impacted and what you did or said to have an impact, you may never know what the impact is. Knowing who was impacted, how many were impacted, and the nature of the impact that you have on the world is not important to satisfying the yearning to be significant. You need only know your intent to be a positive influence on the life of someone else. It is the knowledge that you acted with the purpose of giving and serving with which you should be satisfied. Once you have fulfilled the purpose given to you by the universe, you are not responsible for measuring the impact. You must trust that the forces of the universe will maximize the benefit of your contribution.

CHAPTER 38
SATISFYING THE YEARNING

You will continue to feel the yearning to be significant until you become intimately acquainted with the essence of your being—your soul.

Often my assistant Kevin and I sat in the hearing room awaiting the next case that would be assigned to me. While waiting, we would engage in discussions related to subjects including marriage, rearing children, communication skills, professional speaking, welfare programs, the economy, and the latest political news.

Once while we were in the midst of one such discussion, Carole passed by our opened door. She turned around, stepped into the doorway of the hearing room and asked, "What are you two doing in here?"

Seeking a quick response that wouldn't interrupt the flow of our conversation, I retorted, "Solving the problems of the world."

About to step away and continue on her journey, Carole turned back and urged, "Would you hurry up and get to mine?"

I don't recall the day or the particular subject of conversation or the question from Kevin, if indeed there was a question, but I vividly recall these words to my assistant and friend in our 2003 conversation, "If I were told that today would be my last, I am satisfied." At age fifty-one years, I expected and hoped to live several more, but if that was not to be, I was satisfied. I was satisfied with what I had accomplished by way of an education and a job. I was satisfied with my service to my wife as her husband and with rearing and teaching and being an example for my four children. I was satisfied with my job that allowed me to impact the lives of others, and with the professional speaking that gave me the opportunity to motivate and inspire others. I wanted to speak more, but I was satisfied with what I had done. My third book was in progress although not yet published; nevertheless, I was satisfied. There were things in my life that I wished I had not said or done, but I couldn't change them, so I was satisfied.

Eight years later, I am still married, still teaching and being an example for four children, still giving motivational speeches, still writing, still subject to do and say things that I ought not, and still satisfied.

As I contemplated this chapter, I posed this question to two of my colleagues, "Is your soul satisfied?" One responded, "God, I don't even know what my soul is." The other responded, "I'm content, but I'm not satisfied."

As I write this chapter, what comes to mind are the words of Martin Luther King Jr. on the eve before his assassination in Memphis, Tennessee, "But it really doesn't matter with me now, because I've been to the mountaintop." Dr. King expressed the notion that his soul was satisfied.

Is your soul satisfied?

You will continue to feel the yearning to be significant until you become intimately acquainted with the essence of your being—your soul. When you know your soul, then you'll know what the soul needs to experience fulfillment and satisfaction. The essential element of the soul is love. When that element expands, connects, and impacts, then it is fulfilled.

The soul is satisfied when you utilize your innate talents and abilities. You have been endowed with gifts to contribute to the world, not the whole world necessarily but the portion of the world that you touch. Your soul will not be satisfied unless and until you put your gifts to use. If your strengths and abilities are not utilized, you will always feel a sense of being unfulfilled.

The soul is satisfied when you love without inhibitions. Uninhibited love flows from the soul that is open to express itself in giving and forgiving. Giving and forgiving are acts that love uses to keep the soul free from attachment to things that don't matter or that get in the way of openness—attachments such as materialism, greed, selfishness, envy, begrudging, resentment, and retribution. The soul is satisfied when it can effectively use the attributes of giving and forgiving to let go.

The soul is satisfied when you feel a sense of purpose and are able to answer the self-examining question, Why am I here? So long as this question remains unanswered, you will yearn for the understanding of the meaning of your life. You feel the sense of purpose once you know your individual purpose and you act to fulfill it. You cannot be satisfied if you know your purpose but do nothing toward fulfilling it. On the other hand, it is possible for you to experience purpose based on what you are doing even though you cannot put into words what your individual purpose is.

The soul is satisfied when you live with impact. You can make an impact on your surroundings and the people with whom you interact only when you know who you are and what you have to offer. With the knowledge of your identity and a desire to have an impact, you will seek to know and fulfill your purpose. With the knowledge and understanding of your purpose and a willingness to take action, you will reach out to connect to others. Your soul senses impact from this causal chain of clear Identity, desire for Meaning, understanding Purpose, taking Action, being Connected, and Time on earth well spent. The soul becomes satisfied when it feels the impact; it does not judge its impact by size. Your desire to know the size of your impact signifies a hunger of the ego, not of the soul.

Satisfaction can only come from meaningfulness. If what you are doing and what you acquire has no meaning, you will not be satisfied. You will continue to feel a yearning for something else. You are likely to mistake that soulful yearning for a desire to have more. You then become driven by greed. Greed pushes you to persistently work to possess. When you devote your life to getting rather than to giving, your life will be out of sync with purpose.

You cannot experience satisfaction if you live in contradiction. You cannot live one aspect of your life with purpose and another part out of sync with purpose. If your actions are working against each other, the conflict will produce dissatisfaction. You cannot, for example, serve the needs of homeless children and at the same time invest your money in operations that contribute to the homelessness of children, or destruction of the environment, etc.

When the soul is satisfied, the yearning to be significant is no more.

EPILOGUE
BRINGING IN A NEW YEAR

I affirm that today I am responsible for making each moment of the year meaningful.

Friends and strangers have bid me "Happy New Year," "Have a joyous New Year," and "Have a prosperous New Year." Hearing these good wishes at the end of December is nothing unusual. It has happened every year for all of the years of my life that I can remember. This year I found myself pondering the meaning of the well-wishes. What exactly are these people wishing for me?

If happiness, joy, and prosperity come spontaneously without effort on my part, the fact that someone wishes them for me does nothing to ensure that they will occur. The only thing of which I can be certain is that someone other than me is concerned for my well-being. Still, my emotional, mental, and financial health would be left to chance.

If, on the other hand, emotional highs and financial increase require effort, your wishing happiness, joy, and prosperity for me will not get them for me. I can take pleasure in knowing that you are thinking about me, but I must put forth the effort to obtain the joy and success that I desire to have. All the wishing in the world cannot substitute for my action.

Even if happiness, joy, and prosperity are the result of personal effort, if they are limited resources, by my wishing them for you, I wish against my own success. What you obtain of such limited resources may deprive me of what I seek. Vice versa, when you wish me prosperity, you express hope against your own best interest. Unless, of course, we wish as though we are in a gambling casino hoping and betting against the house. As I sit in a casino and drop coins in the machine of chance, I hope to win, and I hope that my neighbor wins also. She is playing a different machine, so I don't feel that I lose when she wins. But I am at the same time hoping someone loses. I don't want the house to win.

In regards to personal well-being, who or what is The House? And if The House is my source for success, should I not wish for its success as well?

Each moment of your life is the beginning of a new year. It is the start of another 365-day cycle. What will you resolve about the next year of your life?

As I worked on this book, I developed an affirmation to guide me for each new year of life with the understanding that every moment starts a new year. I share my affirmation with the hope that you can make a similar moment-to-moment commitment for yourself.

I choose to believe that happiness, joy, and prosperity are not limited resources. Each person who works for them can obtain them. They are intangible riches that I create through my own effort and actions. As I act for my joy and success, I can hope for yours at the same time and not worry that I will lose if you win. There is no gamble. Every act that I fail to take in my own best interest is just a missed opportunity. The House is an eternal and a universal source of prosperity, joy, and happiness. With every play there is a gain. The House does not need or wish that I lose.

I will take responsibility for my happiness. As it is a transient feeling of euphoria that is dependent on events and circumstances, I will put forth my best effort to be in the places with the people doing the things that make me happy. I will surround myself with happy people and withdraw from those who bring my spirits down. I will wish happiness for others, but I will not carry the burden of their unhappiness.

I will create for myself a permanent state of joy. I will give ear to the voice of my soul and follow his directions. I will live with purpose and love without inhibitions because I know that purpose and love satisfy the soul.

I will take responsibility for my prosperity. I will judge my worth by what I give, not by what I have. I will not compare my success to the success of others nor base my gains on the losses of someone else.

I am in control of my happiness, joy, and prosperity. I need not wait for them to come to me. Indeed, they will not come to me unless I draw them. I need not wait for them to be wished upon me. Doing so puts my happiness, joy, and prosperity in the hands of someone else. Through my own actions I attain happiness, joy, and/or prosperity. Moment by moment, I control my emotional and mental response to my actions, my relationships, and my environment. I am responsible for making the moment meaningful—each moment of my life this year and each year thereafter. It is when I experience meaningfulness in living that I experience happiness, joy, and prosperity.

I wish you many happy days of a joyous and prosperous Every Year—indeed, every moment.

May you have warmth in your igloo, oil in your lamp, and peace in your heart.

- Eskimo Proverb

ACKNOWLEDGEMENTS

Several people contributed to make the development of this book a meaningful experience. I am forever grateful to them all.

Lorene Garrett contributed in the very early stages of the material. When I first started writing about making each moment meaningful, I posted essays on my website in the form of monthly motivational messages. Lorene offered editorial comments and proofreading corrections for every message I posted. Her early contributions saved time and effort when editing and proofreading the book.

Jill Goodmon designed the book cover. She is such a delight to work with.

Chetan Karande offered indirect contribution to the book. First, he contributed by working on redesigning my website to allow me to concentrate on the final revisions of the book. Second, he gave me encouragement to pursue the project when he chose "Making the Moment Meaningful" as the speech I should give to his company's Toastmasters club. The audience's response to the presentation with their follow-up questions confirmed the relevance of the subject matter of the book.

Jacqueline J., Dana C., Winter L., Anton H., and Linnea P.--LaMons all--continued to be loving, patient family members throughout the 5-year project.

Terri Lamon prepared the draft of the manuscript in Microsoft Word format. I still use WordPerfect when I am writing, so I needed Terri's help to transfer and tidy up the manuscript in preparation for the editor.

Winter LaMon worked on the book layout. This is the service I requested of her. It turned out that she had a keen proofreading eye as well.

Sharon White-Senghor provided critical editorial comments. As a result of her work, I had to simplify some concepts, clarify others, and expand still others. She suggested (and I adopted) a major rearrangement of the chapters to make the advice given easier for you, the reader, to follow and apply. I sought Sharon's editorial input because of the beneficial work she did on my first book fifteen years earlier.

Donald N. Williams compensated for my lack of computer skills and prepared the first draft of the manuscript to be circulated three years earlier.

Pamela H. Williams proofread the manuscript. She did most of it during her trip to Honolulu to visit her grandchildren so that the project could be completed on schedule.

Early in my life, I learned the importance and value of relationships with others who help me to accomplish my goals. I have often said that I am grateful for my blindness, which put me in a position to need the help of others. However, the people mentioned above did not help me because I'm blind. They contributed their time and talents to make the moment meaningful.

ABOUT THE AUTHOR

Dana LaMon is a professional speaker who has motivated and inspired audiences around the globe since 1991. He has traveled from Southeast Asia to South Africa and to over thirty states of the United States. His speaking venues have varied from the public classroom of kindergarten students to the private meeting room of corporate executives. He speaks on principles for meaningful living, such as excellence, drive, change, growth and development, overcoming challenges, and diversity and inclusion. He has given over five hundred speeches.

Dana is a member of Toastmasters International, having joined the organization in 1988. He has the unique distinction of being the only Toastmaster with the three designations of Accredited Speaker, World Champion of Public Speaking, and recipient of the President's Citation for outstanding contribution to speaking and leading. He has been honored as Mentor of the Year for his willingness to share his knowledge with others.

Dana LaMon became blind when he was four years old. Using Braille as his primary method for reading and writing, he attended public schools. He graduated with honors from John Marshall High School in Los Angeles, California. After high school, he attended Yale University, where he earned a bachelor's degree in math. He received his law degree from the University of Southern California. He has been a member of the California State Bar since 1978. In 2010 he retired as an administrative law judge after twenty-nine years of service with the California Department of Social Services.

Dana has been married to Jacqueline Jones LaMon since 1983. They have four children. The family makes their home both in Lancaster, California, and Arverne, New York.

www.danalamon.com

Other books by Dana LaMon:

THE SOUL'S MIRROR:
Reflections on the Fullness of Life

THE EXCELLENCE BOOK:
104 Principles for Living and Working

MASTER THE CEREMONIES:
The Emcee's Handbook for Excellence

❖   ❖   ❖

You can order these books and other resources offered by the author by visiting the online store.

For more information about the author's qualifications, speaking availability, books, and recorded presentations, you can contact him at:

ImageWorth
Post Office Box 6108
Lancaster, CA 93539
Tel: (661) 949-7423
E-mail: dana@danalamon.com
www.danalamon.com
www.makingthemomentmeaningful.com

www.makingthemomentmeaningful.com